Learn to Speak Ma

A beginner's guide to mastering conversational Mandarin

BY JADE JIA YING WU

Copyright © 2019 Jade Jia Ying Wu

Written by	Jade Jia Ying Wu
Edited by	Rose Fan Zhang, Ruth Kevess-Cohen
Copy-edited by	Kimberly Newell
Illustration by	Phoebe Tang, Jasmine Jia Wen Xu
Design by	June Pham
Voice Recording by	Rose Fan Zhang, Jian Liu
Cover Design by	Phoebe Tang, June Pham

All rights reserved. This book was self-published by the author Jade Jia Ying Wu under InspirLang Press.

Portions of this book first appeared on the author's website, InspirLang (www.inspirlang.com).

Without limiting the rights under copyright reserved above, no part of this publication may be reproduced, distributed, stored in, or introduced into a retrieval system, or transmitted in any form, or by any means (electronic, mechanical, photocopying, recording, or otherwise), without the written permission of the copyright owner, except in the case of brief quotations embodied in critical reviews and certain other noncommercial uses permitted by the copyright law. For permission requests, contact the author Jade Jia Ying Wu with "Attention: Permissions Coordinator" in the email heading, at the address below.

Jade.Wu@inspirlang.com

Printed in the United States of America
First Printing, 2019
ISBN-13: 978-0-9996946-2-6

To Milok,
who inspired me to start teaching Chinese to my friends, and to all who are looking for a practical guide to learn conversational Mandarin.

Message from the Author

About four years ago, a friend from a business class told me that he was interested in learning Chinese. I told him that I know Chinese and I could teach him. The same day, I went home and created my first website called InspirLang, and began creating podcasts, videos, and other material to teach non-native speakers Mandarin, Cantonese, and Taishanese. In the four years since, these published lessons have gained great success, not only through various online media, but also through one-on-one lessons and group lessons in classrooms.

With the rise of the Chinese economy in recent decades, an abundance of Mandarin textbooks for English speakers have been published. However, as a language enthusiast and teacher, I am always on a journey to find more lively ways to learn and teach a new language. In this book, I created a story between two main characters, An An and Ping Ping, with cartoon illustrations to make learning Chinese more fun and approachable.

This book is based mainly on my experiences teaching Mandarin, learning English and other languages, and discovering cross-cultural differences living in Beijing. It includes questions that most non-native speakers would ask. I believe that language books can be both enjoyable and educational. I hope this book makes learning Mandarin more fun and less intimidating for you.

You know you are learning one of the most difficult languages in the world, but you also know that the most meaningful things in the world are rarely easy. No matter which country you live in, when you are able to give directions to a native Chinese speaker in Mandarin, that is the moment you can celebrate just how much closer you have gotten to someone's heart.

[qiān lǐ zhī xíng, shǐ yú zú xià]
千里之行，始于足下。

A journey of a thousand miles begins with a single step.

– Lao Tzu

Good luck and enjoy your journey of learning Mandarin!

Jade Jia Ying Wu

May, 2019

Table of Contents

Introduction to Mandarin 9

Features of This Book 11

Crash Course 101 on Pinyin – the Mandarin Romanization 14

Chapter 1 19
Hello, my name is…
你好, 我叫… [ní-hǎo, wǒ jiào…]

Chapter 2 30
I would like…
我想要… [wó xiǎng yào…]

Chapter 3 41
Where is…?
…在哪里? […zài ná-lǐ?]

Part I Review 51

Chapter 4 53
I know…
我会… [wǒ huì…]

Chapter 5   64
How do you get to…?
怎么去…? [zěn-me qù…?]

Chapter 6   77
How much is…?
…多少钱? […duō-shǎo qián?]

Part II Review   90

Chapter 7   92
On Sundays I like to…
我星期天喜欢… [wǒ xīng-qī-tiān xǐ-huān…]

Chapter 8   105
Family Members
家人 [jiā-rén]

Chapter 9   114
My birthday is on…
我的生日是… [wǒ-de shēng-rì shì…]

Part III Review   126

Chapter 10 128
Journaling: past, present, and the future
写日记: 过去、现在、将来 [xiě rì-jì: guò-qù、xiàn-zài、jiāng-lái]

List of Interrogative Pronouns 141

Answer Key 142

Introduction to Mandarin

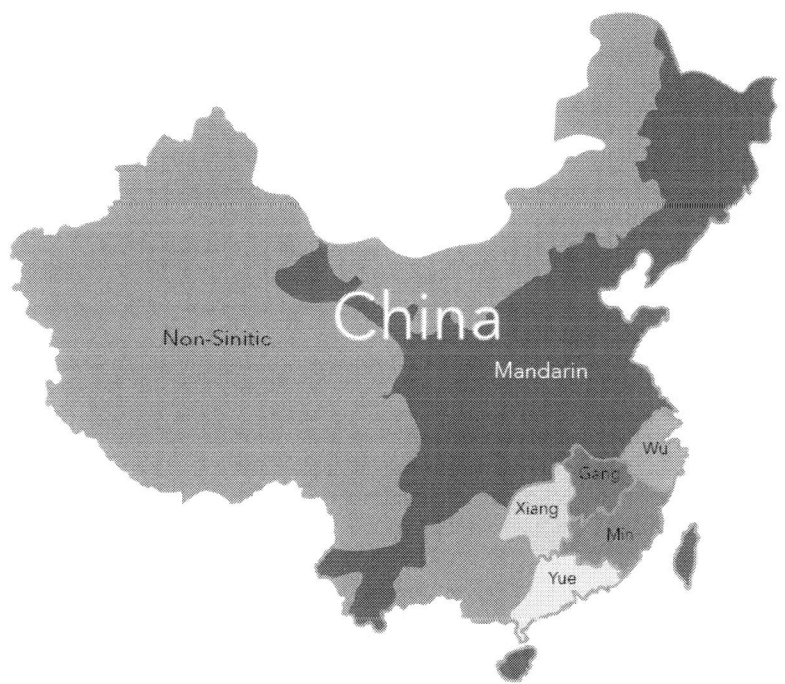

Mandarin, often referred to as Putonghua or literally the common language, is the official language of China. Chinese language class taught in Putonghua (Mandarin) is a requirement as one of the main subjects of the Chinese nine-year compulsory education. Thus, since the founding of the People's Republic of China, every child attending school must learn Putonghua.

What is Mandarin? How is Putonghua different from Mandarin?

The Qing Dynasty, the last dynasty of China, was established by the Manchus (*an ethnic minority group of China*) in 1644. During the Qing Dynasty, Mandarin was only spoken among Chinese officials, thus it is also called 官话 (*guān-huà*), the Official Language.

After the establishment of the People's Republic of China in 1949, Mandarin was renamed as Putonghua, and was chosen as the capital language of China, as a common language that not only officials, but everyone in China, can learn and use to communicate with each other. Ever since then, Mainland China has made a great effort to promote Putonghua and simplified characters.

The Mandarin pronunciation is based on the Beijing dialect, its lexicon is based on the Northern dialect, and its grammar is based on the classics of literary works in modern colloquial Chinese.

Other dialects in China

There are six major dialects in China: Northern 北方 (*includes Beijing dialect*), Yue 粤 (*includes Cantonese*), Xiang 湘 (*includes Hunanese*), Gang 赣 (*includes Nanchang dialect*), Min 闽 (*includes Fujianese*), and Wu 吴 (*includes Shanghainese*). As a matter of fact, there are more than 200 dialects in China, and they often are mutually unintelligible. Therefore, Putonghua, the common language, is used as a bridge language for people who come from different regions in China and speak different dialects.

Because the modern day usage of the term "Mandarin" in English is more common than Putonghua, this book will use "Mandarin" to refer to standard Chinese and the official spoken language of China today.

Features of This Book

Before you jump ahead and start reading this book, here are a few important features of the book that you should know:

Study Goal

The main goal of this book is to help you to learn how to speak basic Mandarin in the fastest way possible. This book focuses on spoken Chinese, and does not require the student to learn how to read or write Chinese characters. However, there is a "Recognizing Chinese Characters" section in each chapter that students can utilize as the first step to learning written Chinese characters.

After learning everything in this book, you should be able to form sentences that are useful in everyday conversation and recognize some of the most commonly used characters.

Audio Track

You can download audio tracks that are supplementary to this book at *www.inspirlang.com/resource* at no additional cost. Audio tracks are provided for all chapters of Vocabulary, Sample Sentences, and Sample Conversation with a 🔊 sign.

Online Flash Cards

You can review and study all of the vocabulary covered in this book by visiting *www.inspirlang.com/resource*.

Vocabulary

In each chapter, there are 3 sections of Vocabulary (A, B and C), all of which are related to the sample topic. Audio tracks are also available online.

Sample Sentences

Similar to the Vocabulary section, there are 3 sections of Sample Sentences in each chapter, all of which are constructed using the Vocabulary. Audio tracks are also available.

Recognizing Chinese Characters

In each chapter, there is a Recognizing Chinese Characters section with 3 characters that the reader should learn to recognize because they are related to the chapter topic and are commonly used in Chinese. There are two types of Chinese characters: simplified Chinese and traditional Chinese. This book will use simplified Chinese characters because they are used as standard Chinese characters in Mainland China.

Sample Conversation

Sample conversations in each chapter are designed to help the reader learn how to talk to a native Mandarin speaker spontaneously by using the vocabulary and sentence structure learned in the given chapter. This is the last part of the audio track in each chapter.

Cultural Insights

At the end of each chapter, you will learn some common Chinese cultural practices such as bargaining in the marketplace and responding to a compliment. That's how you know you are not just learning about the language, but also about the culture and its people.

An-An (ān ān)

Hi, my name is An-An, and I am your narrator and Mandarin teacher throughout this book. I am from Washington, D.C., and I am eight years old (equivalent to twenty-four years old for a human). I have been learning Mandarin with InspirLang for a year, and I am here in Beijing for a computer engineer job interview. Most importantly, I understand your pain of learning a new language as an adult (panda). Trust me, this book will give you a good start with conversational Mandarin and I will show you that Mandarin is not as intimidating as you think it is.

Ping-Ping (píng píng)

This is Ping-Ping, whom I met on my flight from Washington, D.C. to Beijing. This book is focused on how we met on the airplane and spent our first day together in Beijing. She is seven and a half years old. She is from Chengdu and just graduated from college in D.C. Ever since we met, we've gotten along with each other so well. I enjoy it so much when she teaches me Mandarin as well as Chinese culture and traditions. I really think we are a match made in heaven because the combination of our names, píng-píng ān-ān, is a phrase to wish others to be "safe and peaceful."

Crash Course 101 on Pinyin - Mandarin Romanization

Chinese is a tonal language, which means that each character has a fixed pitch pattern. In this way, Chinese is very different from English. To help English and other foreign language speakers understand how to pronounce Chinese characters correctly, Chinese economist and linguist Youguang Zhou (1906-2017) established Hanyu Pinyin in 1958 to romanize Mandarin. This system was officially adopted in 1982 by China as the standard system of romanized spelling for transliterating Chinese (ISO7098). In this book, we will call it Pinyin and use it along with Chinese characters to teach conversational Mandarin. Pinyin is a great tool to help foreign language speakers to pronounce every Chinese character in Mandarin once they learn the initials (consonants), finals (vowels and diphthongs), and tones.

Why are tones so important to learn when studying Chinese?

Because the pitch pattern is an essential part of the meaning of every word. Two characters often have the same pronunciation, but different pitch patterns and therefore different meanings. Here is an example of such a word pair:

The number 4 is considered an unlucky number in Chinese.

But why? That is because "four 四 [sì]" sounds almost exactly the same as the word "death 死 [sǐ]". You see that both "four" and "death" have the same spelling of "si," and the diacritical marks "\" and "∨" above "si" indicate the different tones of the characters. From this example, you can see that the same spelling with different tones can indicate very different meanings.

There are 4 tones in Pinyin. The diacritical marks "¯," "/," "∨," and "\" above the Pinyin vowel (e.g., ā, á, ǎ, à) indicate the fixed tone of that character. See the audio section of the Four Tones on the next page to hear the difference between each tone. Keep listening until you can hear the differences between the four tones. ***Then try to say them yourself.***

4 Tones in Pinyin 🔊

Chinese Character	Pronunciation	Tone	Pronunciation with Tone	Pitch	Translation
吗	ma	neutral	ma	light and unstressed	is a final interrogative particle
妈		1	mā	flat	mom
麻		2	má	rising	numb
马		3	mǎ	rising falling	horse
骂		4	mà	falling	scold

Initials 🔊

b	p	m	f	d
t	n	l	g	k
h	j	q	x	zh
ch	sh	r	z	c
s	y	w		

Finals 🔊

a	o	e	i	u
ü	ai	ei	ui	ao
ou	iu	ie	üe	er
an	en	in	un	un
ang	eng	ing	ong	

Whole Syllables 🔊

zhi	chi	shi	ri	zi
ci	si	yi	wu	yu
ye	yue	yuan	yin	yun
ying				

Pinyin Practice 🔊 *Listen and Repeat.*

b	bāo	bīng	bǐng	bō	bāng
p	piàn	pīng	pīn	pái	pǔ
m	mù	muō	měi	mēng	mí
f	fān	féng	fěi	fù	fèn
d	dū	dān	duān	děng	diū
t	téng	tuī	tái	tǐ	tiē
n	nǐ	néng	nǚ	nù	níng
l	lǐng	lèi	láo	liù	lěng
g	gè	gùn	guò	gèng	guì
k	kùn	kěn	kēng	káng	kào
h	hē	huǒ	hěn	héng	hòu
j	jī	jiào	jiǔ	jiǎ	jū (j+ü)
q	qǐng	qiū	qiǎng	qiè	qú (q+ü)
x	xíng	xiōng	xié	xuān	xūn (x+ün)
zhi	zhí	zhōng	zhàn	zhēn	zhū
chi	chí	chuān	chuāng	chún	chěng
shi	shǐ	shuāi	shàn	shùn	shén
r	rì	rè	róng	ruǎn	rùn
z	zì	zuò	zǒu	zǎo	zàn
c	cì	cān	cù	cèng	cuò
s	sì	suān	sǒng	sài	sū
y	yì	yuān	yōng	yě	yáo
w	wū	wāi	wǎn	wéi	wàng

Chapter 1
Hello, my name is...
你好，我叫…

At 1 a.m., I boarded the airplane to go to Beijing. I am introducing myself to Ping Ping, who is sitting next to me on the flight to Beijing. After reading this chapter, you will be able to greet anyone formally in Mandarin as well as introduce yourself.

你 [nǐ] = you

好 [hǎo] = good; well

你 [ní] + 好 [hǎo] = Hello

As you can see, the way people greet each other in Chinese is similar to saying "you are well" in English.

我 [wǒ] = I; me

叫 [jiào] = to call; to be called

我 [wǒ] + 叫 [jiào] + name = My name is… (lit.* I am called…)

Now you can introduce yourself to others in Mandarin!

我 [wǒ] + 叫 [jiào] + 安安 [ān-ān]
My name is An An.

我 [wǒ] + 叫 [jiào] + 萍萍 [píng-píng]
My name is Ping Ping.

In addition to introducing yourself using "我叫… [wǒ jiào…] My name is…," you can also use "我是… [wǒ shì…] I am…"

> You may notice that when "你-you" is used by itself, it is in the third tone nǐ; however, when it's in the phrase "你好-hello," it's in the second tone ní. That is because, when 2 third tone characters come together (nǐ and hǎo in this case), the first character automatically changes to second tone, ní hǎo.

*lit = literal meaning

我 [wǒ] + 是 [shì] + 安安 [ān-ān]
I am An An.

我 [wǒ] + 是 [shì] + 萍萍 [píng-píng]
I am Ping Ping.

他/她/它 [tā] = he/she/it

Notice that singular third person pronouns are all pronounced as "tā." Because there is no difference between the pronunciations of "he/she/it" in Chinese, you won't be able to tell whether someone is referring to a female or to a male in a conversation where no other hints are supplied other than "tā." In order to know the gender of the third person that is mentioned, you have to explicitly ask or guess based on the context. This is a major reason why the he-she identifier dilemma often happens as Chinese speakers misidentify "he" and "she" when they are speaking English.

Now I would like to add more vocabulary to let Ping Ping know more about me.

Vocabulary A 🔊

美国 [měi-guó] = the United States

中国 [zhōng-guó] = China

英国 [yīng-guó] = England

加拿大 [jiā-ná-dà] = Canada

人 [rén] = people

国 [guó] means "country," and it usually appears at the end of a country name; however, not all country names have the character "国 [guó]," such as "加拿大 [jiā-ná-dà] Canada."

Sample Sentences A 🔊

我是美国人。[wǒ shì měi-guó rén]
I am American. / I am from the U.S.

我是中国人。[wǒ shì zhōng-guó rén]
I am Chinese. / I am from China.

我是加拿大人。[wǒ shì jiā-ná-dà rén]
I am Canadian. / I am from Canada.

Tip:

If you need help finding the right words to fit your scenario, there are many useful dictionary apps that you can download on your phone such as Pleco Chinese Dictionary and Hanping Chinese Dictionary. You should choose one of these dictionaries as a supplement to using this book.

学 [xué] = to learn; to study

我 [wǒ] + 是 [shì] + 学 [xué] + field of study + 的 [de] = I study…

工程 [gōng-chéng] = engineering

我 [wǒ] + 是 [shì] + 学 [xué] +工程 [gōng-chéng] + 的 [de] = I study engineering.

The "是…的 [shì…de] structure" is very commonly used in Chinese to specify a particular action. It can be used in many different situations, and it's not restricted to discussing fields of studies.

Now that we've learned the structure of telling others your background, let's learn more occupations to understand what Ping Ping studies.

Vocabulary B 🔊

工程 [gōng-chéng] = engineering

设计 [shè-jì] = designing

教育学 [jiào-yù xué] = education; pedagogy

中文 [zhōng-wén] = Chinese (language)

Sample Sentences B 🔊

我是学工程的。[wǒ shì xué gōng-chéng de]
I study/studied engineering.

我是学设计的。[wǒ shì xué shè-jì de]
I study/studied designing.

我是学教育学的。[wǒ shì xué jiào-yù xué de]
I study/studied education.

我是学中文的。[wǒ shì xué zhōng-wén de]
I study/studied Chinese.

Vocabulary C 🔊

工程师 [gōng-chéng-shī] = engineer

设计师 [shè-jì-shī] = designer

老师 [lǎo-shī] = teacher

学生 [xué-shēng] = student

Note

Did you notice the 师 (shī) after the translation "engineering 工程 (gōng-chéng)" and "designing 设计 (shè-jì)?" The character 师 (shī) means mastery in a certain field and it resembles the "…er," "…ist," or "…ant" in English coming after fields of study such as "teacher," "journalist," and "accountant."

Sample Sentences C 🔊

我是工程师。[wǒ shì gōng-chéng-shī]
I am (an) engineer.

我是设计师。[wǒ shì shè-jì-shī]
I am (a) designer.

我是老师。[wǒ shì lǎo-shī]
I am (a) teacher.

Recognizing Chinese Characters

Remember, your goal in this book is to get comfortable speaking Mandarin to native speakers. You don't need to worry about writing all the characters yet, but learning to recognize these most frequently used characters in each chapter will help you to learn how to write characters in the future.

1. 我 [wǒ] = I; me
2. 你 [nǐ] = you
3. 人 [rén] = person; people

Sample Conversation 🔊

Ping Ping: 你好！[ní-hǎo!]
Hello!

An An: 你好，我叫安安。[ní-hǎo, wǒ jiào ān-ān]
Hi, my name is An An.

你是哪里人? [nǐ shì ná-lǐ rén?]
Where are you from? / What is your nationality?
哪里 [ná-lǐ] = where

Ping Ping: 我是四川人。[wǒ shì sì-chuān rén]
I am from Sichuan/Szechuan.

安安，你是做什么的? [ān-ān, nǐ shì zuò shén-me de?]
What do you do? / What is your job, An An?
什么 [shén-me] = what

An An: 我是工程师。[wǒ shì gōng-chéng-shī]
I am an engineer.

Cultural Insights

1. In Chinese, there are two terms used to address "you"
   你 [nǐ] = you (informal)
   您 [nín] = you (formal and honorific)

2. To someone that you are meeting or talking to for the first time, you should always address the other person as 您 (nín). For example, even when you are on a cellphone conversation with a waiter who is taking your restaurant reservation, you should use 您 (nín) to show your politeness even though he/she is the one serving you.

3. You should also address someone with 您 (nín) if the other person is older than you.

In this book, I will only be using the informal term 你 (nǐ) in all situations because it's more common. However, you will have the option to choose between informal and formal terms based on your audience.

Chapter 1 Exercises

1. What is the literal meaning of "hello 你好 (ní-hǎo)" in Chinese?

   ....

2. Translate the following sentences:

   [wǒ shì měi-guó rén]
   我是美国人。
   ....

   [nǐ shì zhōng-guó rén?]
   你是中国人?
   ....

   [wǒ shì jiā-ná-dà ......]
   我是加拿大人。
   I am from Canada.

3. Fill in the blanks according to the translation.

   A: What do you study?

   B: [...... .... gōng-chéng de]
   我是学工程的。
   I study engineering.

A: What is your occupation?

B: [...... ...... gōng-chéng-shī]
我是工程师。
I am an engineer.

Chapter 2
I would like...
我想要...

At 2 a.m., an hour after boarding, Ping Ping and I are requesting different airline meals from the flight attendant. After reading this chapter, you will be able to use this sentence structure to order food at a Chinese restaurant and will know the names of some Chinese dishes.

想 [xiǎng] = to want to...

要 [yào] = to need...; to have to...

想要 [xiǎng yào] = would like

我 [wó*] + 想要 [xiǎng yào] + noun = I would like...

*Here, wǒ became wó again because the following character 想 (xiǎng) is a third tone syllable.

Now, let's start with learning beverage names and how to order them!

Vocabulary A 🔊

水 [shuǐ] = water

茶 [chá] = tea

可乐 [kě-lè] = Coke (or cola)

咖啡 [kā-fēi] = coffee

橙汁 [chéng-zhī] = orange juice

奶茶 [nǎi-chá] = milk tea

珍珠奶茶 [zhēn-zhū nǎi-chá] = bubble tea (lit. pearl milk tea)

Sample Sentence A

我想要可乐。[wó xiǎng yào kě-lè]
I would like a Coke.

我想要水。[wó xiǎng yào shuǐ]
I would like a water.

我想要咖啡。[wó xiǎng yào kā-fēi]
I would like a coffee.

我想要茶。[wó xiǎng yào chá]
I would like a tea.

Vocabulary B

鸡肉 [jī-ròu] = chicken (meat)

牛肉 [niú-ròu] = beef (meat)

猪肉 [zhū-ròu] = pork (meat)

海鲜 [hǎi-xiān] = seafood

土豆 [tǔ-dòu] = potato

饭 [fàn] = rice

面 [miàn] = noodles

> " You may be puzzled that there is no indication of "a" here when we say "I would like (a) coke 我想要可乐 (wó xiǎng-yào kě-lè)" in Chinese. To explicitly express one unit of something, you will have to add in a classifier, or measure word, which I will explain later in Section C of this chapter.

饺子 [jiǎo-zi] = dumpling

锅贴 [guō-tiē] = potsticker (pan-fried dumpling)

Sample Sentence B 🔊

我想要牛肉饭。[wó xiǎng yào niú-ròu fàn]
I would like beef (with) rice.

我想要海鲜面。[wó xiǎng yào hǎi-xiān miàn]
I would like seafood noodles.

你好, 我想要鸡肉土豆。
[ní-hǎo, wó xiǎng yào jī-ròu tǔ-dòu]
Hi, I would like chicken (and mashed) potatoes.

我想要锅贴。[wó xiǎng yào guō-tiē]
I would like potstickers.

Cultural Insights

In many casual restaurants when a waiter addresses a female customer, he may use "美女 (méi*-nǚ) pretty woman" to a female customer, or "帅哥 (shuài-gē) handsome man" to a male customer. It is not necessarily flirty, and it only happens in a casual restaurant.

Now, let's take a look at some examples of common classifiers.

美* [měi] = beautiful, měi becomes méi when followed by a third tone syllable

Vocabulary C 🔊

一 [yī] = one

一个 [yí-gè] = one (person, object, or abstract idea); generic classifier

一份 [yí-fèn] = one (serving or share)

一杯 [yì-bēi] = one (cup)

一碗 [yì-wǎn] = one (bowl)

一个人 [yí-gè rén] = one person

一个美国人 [yí-gè měi-guó rén] = one American (person)

一份锅贴 [yí-fèn guō-tiē] = one serving of potstickers

一杯茶 [yì-bēi chá] = one cup of tea

一碗牛肉面 [yì-wǎn niú-ròu miàn] = one bowl of beef noodles

This is another tone change besides the third tone change rule, where "nǐ-hǎo" becomes "ní-hǎo". When "一 (yī) one" is used by itself, it's in first tone. When it's before a fourth tone, it becomes second tone.

Tone Change Rules (Tone Sandhi) we learned:

- When two 3rd tone characters come together, tones (3)(3) become (2)(3)
- When "一 (yī) one" is used, if the next character is 4th tone, then (yī) becomes second tone (yí); otherwise, (yī) becomes fourth tone (yì).

In Chinese, a classifier, or measure word is needed to quantify or specify the amount of something. It functions similarly to the "bottle" in the phrase "a bottle of water", the "piece" in "two pieces of paper," and "pound" in "three pounds of beef" in English. There are many classifiers in Chinese, and they usually refer to a specific category such as shape and functionality. However, there is a generic classifier 个 (gè) that you can use when you don't know which appropriate classifier you should apply. Using 个 (gè) may not be always right, but people will understand you.

Sample Sentences C 🔊

我想要一个牛肉饭。[wó xiǎng yào yí-gè niú-ròu fàn]
I would like a beef with rice.

你好，我想要一碗牛肉饭。[ní-hǎo, wó xiǎng yào yì-wǎn niú-ròu fàn]
Hi/Excuse me, I would like a bowl of beef rice.

我想要一碗海鲜面。[wó xiǎng yào yì-wán* hǎi-xiān miàn]
I would like a bowl of seafood noodles.

碗 [wǎn] becomes wán when followed by a third tone syllable

我想要一杯奶茶。[wó xiǎng yào yì-bēi nǎi-chá]
I would like a cup of milk tea.

我想要一杯水。[wó xiǎng yào yì-bēi shuǐ]
I would like a cup of water.

Grammar Takeaway – Subject-Verb-Object (S.V.O.) is the most basic word order in Chinese. As you may have noticed, all of the examples that we have encountered so far are simple statements that fall into the subject-verb-object pattern, and they are very similar to English. However, in sentences with interrogative pronouns (what, where, why, when, which, how), the most basic pattern is subject-verb-question. You can take a look at the example below.

什么 [shén-me] = what
你 [ní] + 想要 [xiǎng yào] + 什么 [shén-me] ? = What would you like?

Recognizing Chinese Characters

1. 个 [gè] = generic classifier; classifier for people, objects, and abstract ideas
2. 水 [shuǐ] = water
3. 茶 [chá] = tea

Sample Conversation 🔊

Flight Attendant: 您好，请问您想要什么？ [nín-hǎo, qǐng-wèn nín xiǎng yào shén-me?]
Hi, what would you like please?

An An: 我想要一份牛肉饭，一杯茶。 [wó xiǎng yào yí-fèn niú-ròu fàn, yì-bēi chá]
I would like beef with rice, (and) a cup of tea.

Flight Attendant: 好的，请稍等。 [hǎo-de, qǐng shāo děng]
Okay, please wait for a second.

An An: 谢谢。 [xiè-xiè]
Thank you.

> Remember, in any formal settings, you can use 您(nín) instead of 你 (nǐ) to address the other person.

Cultural Insights | Chinese Titles

As we have discussed before, some of the casual ways to address someone are "美女 (méi-nǚ) pretty woman" and "帅哥 (shuài-gē) handsome man." However, you will not be able to use them in a formal setting; instead, you can use the following titles:

先生 [xiān-shēng] = Mr. ; sir

小姐 [xiáo*-jiě] = Miss

女士 [nǚ-shì] = Ms.

太太 [tài-tai] = Mrs.

*小 [xiǎo], becomes xiáo when followed by a third tone syllable

师傅 [shī-fù] is the title for a specialized worker such as a plumber or driver

In English, we mention the last name after the title, for example, Mr. Smith and Ms. Chan. However, in Chinese we always mention last names first. For example, 王先生 (wáng xiān-shēng) for Mr. Wang and 王小姐 (wáng xiáo-jiě) for Miss Wang.

In Chinese culture, last names are so important and highly recognized because they represent the glory of a clanship and family history. Today, some families still keep a genealogical record – 族谱 (zú-pǔ), which records all names of ancestors in the kinship for later generations to trace back their lineage. To understand it in a contemporary way, it's similar to people creating elaborate family trees online and buying DNA testing kits to find out their lineage and where they come from. 族谱 (zú-pǔ) is not typical for a Chinese family today, but some families still maintain it.

Chapter 2 Exercise

1. What is the phrase of "I would like…" when you want to order something?

   ....

2. What is the generic classifier that you need to add between a number and a noun to quantify an object?

   ....

3. What is missing from this sentence?

   [ní .... shén-me?] = What would you like?

4. Translate the following sentences:

   [wó xiǎng yào nǎi-chá]
   我想要奶茶。

   ....

   [ní xiǎng yào niú-ròu miàn?]
   你想要牛肉面?

   ....

5. Fill in the blanks.

   A: 你想要什么？ [ní xiǎng yào ....?]
   What would you like?

   B: 我想要一杯咖啡。[..... .... yì-bēi kā-fēi]
   I would like a cup of coffee.

Chapter 3
Where is...?
...在哪里?

At 3 p.m., after a 14-hour flight, I finally arrived at the Beijing Capital International Airport. After filling out the arrival card and going through customs, I hired a taxi to go to the company where I was going to have my job interview. After reading this chapter, you will be able to ask for directions and navigate in Chinese, and will know about some Chinese transportation network apps similar to Uber and Lyft in the U.S.

A beginner's guide to mastering conversational Mandarin Chinese

哪里 [ná*-lǐ] / 哪儿 [nǎ-er] = where

哪 [nǎ] becomes ná when followed by a third tone syllable

…在哪里 […zài ná-lǐ] / …在哪儿 […zài nǎ-er] = where is…(at)

As you can see, there are two ways to express "where:" 哪里 (ná-lǐ) and 哪儿 (nǎ-er). They have no difference in meaning, although 哪里 (ná-lǐ) is more common in Southern China and 哪儿 (nǎ-er) is more common in Northern China. 儿 (er) is a suffix that is used by many northern dialect speakers when they speak Mandarin. There are some patterns that explain when to apply the suffix 儿 (er), but its application can seem very random to a non-native speaker. In this book, we will be using 哪里 (ná-lǐ) to avoid any confusion.

Let's start learning some location names in order to ask someone for directions.

Vocabulary A

洗手间 [xí*-shǒu-jiān] = bathroom

洗 [xǐ] becomes xí when followed by a third tone syllable

机场 [jī-chǎng] = airport

公交车站 [gōng-jiāo-chē zhàn] = bus stop

地铁站 [dì-tiě zhàn] = subway station

Sample Sentence A 🔊

洗手间在哪里? [xí-shǒu-jiān zài ná-lǐ?]
Where is the bathroom (at)?

请问公交车站在哪里? [qǐng-wèn gōng-jiāo-chē zhàn zài ná-lǐ?]
Where is the bus stop (at) please?
请问 [qǐng-wèn] = please; excuse me, may I ask...

你好, 请问地铁站在哪里? [ní-hǎo, qǐng-wèn dì-tiě zhàn zài ná-lǐ?]
Hi, where is the subway station (at) please?

你好, 请问机场在哪里? [ní-hǎo, qǐng-wèn jī-chǎng zài ná-lǐ?]
Hi, where is the airport (at) please?

As you may have seen, adding 请问 (qǐng-wèn) before the question shows the speaker's politeness, similar to saying "excuse me" in English before asking someone a question.

Vocabulary B 🔊

这里 [zhè-lǐ] / 这儿 [zhè-er] = here

那里 [nà-lǐ] / 那儿 [nà-er] = there

地方 [dì-fāng] = place

这个地方 [zhè-gè dì-fāng] = this place

那个地方 [nà-gè dì-fāng] = that place

Now let's implement the sentence structure that we just learned.

Sample Sentences B

这个地方在哪里? [zhè-gè dì-fāng zài ná-lǐ?]
Where is this place (at)?

那个地方在哪里? [nà-gè dì-fāng zài ná-lǐ?]
Where is that place (at)?

你在哪里? [nǐ zài ná-lǐ?]
Where are you?

我想去这个地方。 [wó xiǎng qù zhè-gè dì-fāng]
I want to go to this place.

我想去那里。 [wó xiǎng qù nà-lǐ]
I want to go there.

> We will continue to use 这里 (zhè-lǐ) and 那里 (nà-lǐ) instead of 这儿 (zhè-er) and 那儿 (nà-er) in this chapter and in the following chapters throughout this book.

Note

Remember how to say "I would like" in Chinese?
想要 [xiǎng yào] = would like
想 [xiǎng] = want to

As we have learned how to ask for directions, let's take a look at how we can navigate in Mandarin.

Vocabulary C 🔊

前面 [qián-miàn] front
后面 [hòu-miàn] back
左边 [zuǒ-biān] left side
右边 [yòu-biān] right side

在 A 前面 [zài A qián-miàn] in front of A
在 A 后面 [zài A hòu-miàn] behind A
在 A 左边 [zài A zuǒ-biān] on the left side of A
在 A 右边 [zài A yòu-biān] on the right side of A

东 [dōng] east
南 [nán] south
西 [xī] west
北 [běi] north

在 A 东边 [zài A dōng-biān] on the east side of A
在 A 南边 [zài A nán-biān] on the south side of A
在 A 西边 [zài A xī-biān] on the west side of A
在 A 北边 [zài A běi-biān] on the north side of A

Sample Sentences C 🔊

我在地铁站前面。[wǒ zài dì-tiě zhàn qián-miàn]
I am in front of the subway station.

我在公交车站后面。[wǒ zài gōng-jiāo-chē zhàn hòu-miàn]
I am behind the bus stop.

我在机场北边。[wǒ zài jī-cháng* běi-biān]
I am on the north side of the airport.

> 场 [chǎng] becomes cháng when followed by a third tone syllable

我在你西边。[wǒ zài nǐ xī-biān]
I am to the west of you.

Recognizing Chinese Characters

1. 这 [zhè] = this
2. 那 [nà] = that
3. 哪 [nǎ] = where

Sample Conversation 🔊

Driver: 您好，请问您在哪里? [nín-hǎo, qǐng-wèn nín zài ná-lǐ?]
  Hi, where are you please?

An An: 我在机场南边。[wǒ zài jī-chǎng nán-biān]
  I am on the south side of the airport.

Driver: 好的。[hǎo de]
  Okay.

After the Didi driver picks me up from the airport.

Driver: 请问您要去哪里? [qǐng-wèn nín yào qù ná-lǐ?]
  Where do you need to go please?

An An: 我想去这个地方。[wó xiǎng qù zhè-gè dì-fāng]
  I would like to go to this place.

Driver: 好的。[hǎo de]
  Okay.

Note

One of the most popularly-used transportation apps in China is Didi Chuxing, or Didi in short.

Cultural Insights | Navigating with your taxi driver in Beijing

As we have mentioned, Didi is the most popular taxi app in China today. It is available in both Chinese and English, and it's similar to Uber, which is used in many other countries. Because the subway systems in China (including Beijing, Shanghai, and Hong Kong) do not operate 24 hours a day, it is inevitable to find yourself taking a Didi or other taxi service when you are out after 11 p.m. Here are some things to be careful of when you take a Didi:

1. People from Beijing are very oriented to cardinal directions, like north, south, east, and west when they are navigating, while other cities use relative directions, like left, right, front, and back.

2. In Beijing, when your Didi driver asks you for your location before picking you up, he/she will be expecting you to provide cardinal directions like "southeast" and "northeast" from a certain building.

Chapter 3 Exercise

1. What is the Mandarin preposition that is similar to "at" in English?
   ....

2. How would you ask someone where he/she is?
   ....

3. Are both …在哪里 […zài ná-lǐ] and …在哪儿 […zài nǎ-er] acceptable to ask "where is…at?"
   ....

4. Translate the following sentences:

   我在地铁站。[wǒ zài dì-tiě zhàn]
   ....

   我在地铁站前面。 [wǒ zài dì-tiě zhàn qián-miàn]
   ....

   我在公交车站右边。[wǒ zài gōng-jiāo-chē zhàn yòu-biān]
   ....

   我在公交车站东边。[wǒ zài gōng-jiāo-chē zhàn dōng-biān]
   ....

5. Fill in the blanks.

   A: [...... .... ná-lǐ?] 你想去哪里? Where do you want to go?

   B: [...... .... xí-shǒu-jiān] 我想去洗手间。I would like to go to the bathroom.

Part I Review

- To greet another person, you say "你好 (ní-hǎo) hello."
- To address someone formally, you should use 您 (nín) instead of 你 (nǐ).
- To tell someone what your name is, you say "我叫… (wǒ jiào…) my name is…."
- To tell someone what your career is, you say "我是… (wǒ shì…) I am (a)…."
- To let someone know where you are from, you can state "我是…人 (wǒ shì…rén) I am from…."
- To tell someone what you study, you can tell them "我是学…的 (wǒ shì xué…de) I study…."
- To order at a restaurant or cafe, you can say "我想要…(wó xiǎng yào…) I would like…."
- To find out where something is located, you can ask "…在哪里 (…zài ná-lǐ) where is…?"
- To show politeness when you ask someone a question, you can add "请问 (qǐng-wèn) please" at the beginning of the sentence.
- Here = 这里 (zhè-lǐ) | There (nà-lǐ) = 那里
- This = 这个 (zhè-gè) | That (nà-gè) = 那个

Sample Paragraph

你好，我叫大卫。我是美国人。我是学中文的。我想去北京。
[ní-hǎo, wǒ jiào dà-wèi。wǒ shì měi-guó rén。wǒ shì xué zhōng-wén de。wó xiǎng qù běi-jīng。]

English Translation:
Hi, my name is David. I am from the United States. I study Chinese. I want to go to Beijing.

Sample Exercise

Translate the following sentences.

[wǒ shì sì-chuān rén] 我是四川人。

....

[...... ....] 我想要一碗海鲜面。
I would like a bowl of seafood noodles.

[...... ....?] 你在哪里?
Where are you?

Chapter 4
I know...
我会...

At 4 p.m., I arrived at Alipanda's Beijing headquarters for my computer engineer job interview. While having a conversation with my interviewer, I explained my job-related skills and my years of experience. After reading this chapter, you will be able to tell someone about your expertise and years of work experience.

A beginner's guide to mastering conversational Mandarin Chinese

Vocabulary A 🔊

中文 [zhōng-wén] = Chinese (language)

普通话 [pǔ-tōng-huà] = Mandarin/Putonghua

英语 [yīng-yǔ] = English (language)

法语 [fá*-yǔ] = French (language)   法 [fǎ] becomes fá when followed by a third tone syllable

西班牙语 [xī-bān-yá-yǔ] = Spanish (language)

编程 [biān-chéng] = to program

Let's take a look at how to express your skills with the following sentence structure:

会 [huì] = to know (a skill)

用 [yòng] = to use

我 [wǒ] + 会 [huì] + skill = I know…

我 [wǒ] + 会 [huì] + 用 [yòng] + application = I know how to use…

Sample Sentences A 🔊

我会中文。[wǒ huì zhōng-wén]
I know Chinese.

我会西班牙语。[wǒ huì xī-bān-yá-yǔ]
I know Spanish.

我会编程。[wǒ huì biān-chéng]
I know how to program.

我会用Javascript。[wǒ huì yòng Javascript]
I know how to use Javascript.

我会用Javascript、Python、和Swift。[wǒ huì yòng Javascript、Python、hé Swift]
I know how to use Javascript, Python, and Swift.

> Note that 和 (hé) serves as the conjunction "and" here. It is a conjunction to connect nouns together, but not sentences.

Let's learn some Chinese numbers and use them to describe your years of work experience in section B.

Vocabulary B 🔊

1. 一 [yī]
2. 二 [èr]
3. 三 [sān]
4. 四 [sì]
5. 五 [wǔ]
6. 六 [liù]
7. 七 [qī]
8. 八 [bā]
9. 九 [jiǔ]
10. 十 [shí]

Let's use the names of foods that we learned from Chapter 2 to form new sentences with numbers!

我是一个老师。[wǒ shì yí-gè lǎo-shī]
I am a teacher.

你是一个学生？[nǐ shì yí-gè xué-shēng?]
You are a student?

> Note
> Remember that the tone change rule of 一 (yī) we learned from the last chapter is applied here.

我想要一碗牛肉饭。[wó xiǎng yào yì-wǎn niú-ròu fàn]
I would like one bowl of beef with rice.

我想要三碗鸡肉拉面。[wó xiǎng yào sān-wǎn jī-ròu lā-miàn]
I would like three bowls of chicken ramen.

我想要两杯咖啡。[wó xiǎng yào liǎng-bēi kā-fēi]
I would like two cups of coffee.

Question: Why do you say "两杯 (liǎng-bēi)" instead of "二杯 (èr-bēi)" for "two cups of coffee?"

The number 2 is an exception in Chinese. When you are trying to quantify something with the number 2, you would always use "两 (liǎng)." For example, when you are trying to say "two cups of coffee," "two people," "two o'clock," or even "two dollars," you would say "两 (liǎng)." When you are counting "1, 2, 3, 4...," you would use "二 (èr)."

Now, let's learn some names of popular Chinese companies to be used in sample sentences.

Vocabulary C 🔊

阿里巴巴 [ā-lǐ-bā-bā] = Alibaba

亚马逊 [yà-mǎ-xùn] = Amazon

百度 [bǎi-dù] = Baidu (similar to Google)

淘宝 [táo-bǎo] = Taobao (e-commerce)

京东 [jīng-dōng] = JD.com (e-commerce)

美团 [měi-tuán] = Meituan-Dianping (similar to the combination of Yelp and Groupon)

工作 [gōng-zuò] = work

工作了 [gōng-zuò le] = worked

年 [nián] = year

在 [zài] + location + 工作了 [gōng-zuò le] + number + 年 [nián] = worked at…for…years

在阿里巴巴工作了一年 [zài ā-lǐ-bā-bā gōng-zuò le yì nián] = worked at Alibaba for one year

You will learn more about conjugations later in Chapter 10.

Sample Sentences C 🔊

我在亚马逊工作了三年。[wǒ zài yà-mǎ-xùn gōng-zuò le sān nián]
I worked at Amazon for three years.

我在百度工作了两年。[wǒ zài bǎi-dù gōng-zuò le liǎng nián]
I worked at Baidu for two years.

我在淘宝工作了五年。[wǒ zài táo-bǎo gōng-zuò le wǔ nián]
I worked at Taobao for five years.

你在亚马逊工作了五年? [nǐ zài yà-mǎ-xùn gōng-zuò le wǔ nián?]
You worked at Amazon for five years?

你在亚马逊工作了五年吗？ [nǐ zài yà-mǎ-xùn gōng-zuò le wǔ nián ma?]
Did you work at Amazon for five years?

Recognizing Chinese Characters

1. 三 [sān] = three
2. 在 [zài] = at
3. 了 [le] = past participle

> **Note**
> To turn a statement into a yes-or-no question, you can simply add 吗 (ma) at the end of your statement.

Sample Conversation 🔊

An An: 你好，我叫安安。[ní-hǎo, wǒ jiào ān-ān]
Hi, my name is An An.

Interviewer: 你好，安安。你会什么语言？ [ní-hǎo, ān-ān。nǐ huì shén-me yǔ-yán?]
Hi, An An. What languages do you know?

An An: 我会英语和一点点中文。[wǒ huì yīng-yǔ hé yì-dián*-diǎn zhōng-wén]
I know English and a little Chinese.

Interviewer: 你的中文很好。[nǐ de zhōng-wén hén* hǎo]
Your Chinese is very good.

点 [diǎn] = a little, diǎn becomes dián when followed by a third tone syllable

很 [hěn] = very, hěn becomes hén when followed by a third tone syllable

An An:	哪里哪里。[ná-lǐ ná-lǐ] Thank you. (lit: where?)	**Note** This phenomenon will be explained in Cultural Insights on the next page.
Interviewer:	安安，你是学什么的？[ān-ān, nǐ shì xué shén-me de?] What do you study, An An?	
An An:	我是学编程的。[wǒ shì xué biān-chéng de] I study programming.	
Interviewer:	你会什么编程语言？[nǐ huì shén-me biān-chéng yǔ-yán?] What programming languages do you know?	
An An:	我会Javascript、Swift、和Python。[wǒ huì Javascript、Swift、hé Python] I know Javascript, Swift, and Python.	
Interviewer:	你以前在哪里工作？[ní yǐ-qián zài ná-lǐ gōng-zuò?] Where did you work before?	
An An:	我在亚马逊工作了三年。[wǒ zài yà-mǎ-xùn gōng-zuò le sān nián] I worked at Amazon for three years.	

Cultural Insights | Responding to compliments in Chinese

Humility is considered a virtue in many East Asian cultures, and therefore it is considered polite to be humble by downplaying yourself when someone gives you a compliment. There are many Chinese proverbs that praise humility such as "The more noble, the more humble." In Chapter 2's Sample Conversation, we have learned that "谢谢 (xiè-xiè)" is the direct translation of "thank you." However, when someone gives you a compliment, you can simply say "哪里哪里 (ná-lǐ ná-lǐ)." Although it literally means "where is it," it implies the speaker's humility by meaning "In what way am I good enough?"

You may feel a little uneasy when you know you have put a lot of effort into achieving something but have to downplay yourself, but here are two very practical benefits of being humble:

1. To make yourself seem less threatening to others.

2. When you actually make a mistake, no one can blame you because you never claimed to be good at it.

Chapter 4 Exercise

1. What is the verb in Mandarin when you want to express your skill as "I know…?"
   ....

2. When quantifying something, the number two is an exception. Instead of saying 二 (èr), what do you say when you want to quantify "two" of something?
   ....

3. How do you say "he would like two cups of coffee" in Mandarin?
   ....

4. Translate the following sentences.
   [wǒ zài zhè-lǐ gōng-zuò le liǎng nián]
   我在这里工作了两年。

   ....

   [nǐ zài zhè-gè dì-fāng gōng-zuò le wǔ nián?]
   你在这个地方工作了五年?

   ....

5. Can you read the following numbers in Chinese?

[yī]	[sān]	[wǔ]	[qī]	[jiǔ]
一	三	五	七	九
……	……	……	……	……

[èr]	[sì]	[liù]	[bā]	[shí]
二	四	六	八	十
……	……	……	……	……

Chapter 5
How do you get to...?
怎么去...?

At 5 p.m., I finished my interview at Alipanda and decided to take a subway to go to the Forbidden City. I will also introduce you to other tourist attractions in Beijing.

After reading this chapter, you will be able to say ordinal numbers in Mandarin and more transition words to apply them to giving directions, and will know about appropriate social interactions on the Beijing subway.

Now, let's take a look at the sentence structure for asking how to get to a place.

怎么 [zěn-me] = how

去 [qù] = to go

怎么 [zěn-me] + 去 [qù] = how to go (to)…

怎么 [zěn-me] + 去 [qù] + 故宫 [gù-gōng]? = How do you go to the Forbidden City?

Vocabulary A 🔊

故宫 [gù-gōng] = Forbidden City

长城 [cháng-chéng] = the Great Wall

天安门 [tiān-ān-mén] = Tian'anmen (Square)

雍和宫 [yōng-hé-gōng] = Yonghegong Lama Temple

天坛 [tiān-tán] = Temple of Heaven

奥林匹克公园 [ào-lín-pǐ-kè gōng-yuán] = Olympic Park

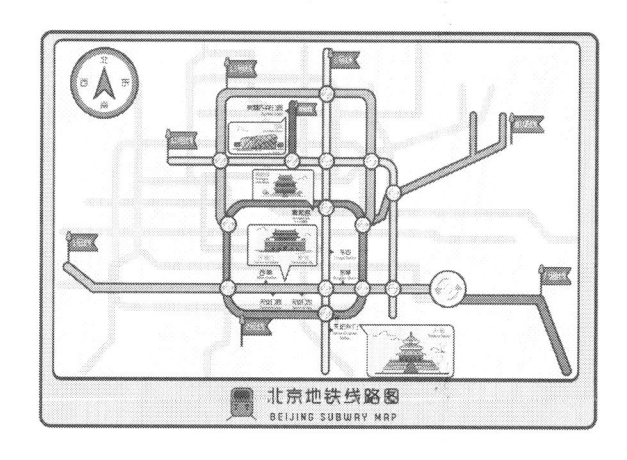

Sample Sentence A 🔊

怎么去故宫? [zěn-me qù gù-gōng?]
How do you go to the Forbidden City?

怎么去长城？ [zěn-me qù cháng-chéng?]
How do you go to the Great Wall?

请问, 怎么去天安门？ [qǐng-wèn, zěn-me qù tiān-ān-mén?]
Excuse me, how do you go to Tian'anmen?

你好, 请问怎么去这个地方？ [ní-hǎo, qǐng-wèn zěn-me qù zhè-gè dì-fāng?]
Hi, how do you go to this place, please?

你好, 请问怎么去奥林匹克公园？ [ní-hǎo, qǐng-wèn zěn-me qù ào-lín-pǐ-kè gōng-yuán?]
Hi, how do you go to Olympic Park, please?

> As we learned from Chapter 3, we can always use …在哪里 (…zài ná-lǐ) to rephrase your question and make it "where is…?" When discussing direction to a place, you may hear both cardinal and ordinal numbers.

Do you still remember Chinese numbers 1-10?

1. 一 [yī]

2. 二 [èr]

3. 三 [sān]

4. 四 [sì]

5. 五 [wǔ]

6. 六 [liù]

7. 七 [qī]

8. 八 [bā]

9. 九 [jiǔ]

10. 十 [shí]

Ordinal numbers in Chinese are easy once you learn the cardinal numbers. To state an ordinal number, you can simply add the prefix 第 (dì) before the cardinal number. Take a look at the following examples:

第 [dì] + 1 [yī] = first

第 [dì] + 2 [èr] = second

第 [dì] + 3 [sān] = third

When taking a subway or bus, you will often hear people say …号线 (hào xiàn) to indicate the route.
number + 号线 [hào xiàn] = line #

1 [yī] + 号线 [hào xiàn] = line 1

6 [liù] + 号线 [hào xiàn] = line 6

地铁 [dì-tiě] + 1 [yī] + 号线 [hào xiàn] = Subway Line 1

6 [liù] + 路 [lù] + 公交车 [gōng-jiāo-chē] = Road 6 bus; No. 6 bus

Vocabulary B 🔊

第一 [dì-yī] = first

第二 [dì-èr]= second

第三 [dì-sān] = third

第四 [dì-sì] = fourth

第五 [dì-wǔ] = fifth

第六 [dì-liù] = sixth

第七 [dì-qī] = seventh

第八 [dì-bā] = eighth

第九 [dì-jiǔ] = ninth

第十 [dì-shí] = tenth

然后 [rán-hòu] = then

最后 [zuì-hòu] = finally

上车 [shàng-chē] = to get on a vehicle

下车 [xià-chē] = to get off from a vehicle

换乘 [huàn-chéng] = to transfer (among vehicles)

走 [zǒu] = to walk

Sentence Structure Takeaway

在…上车 [zài…shàng-chē] = to get on a vehicle at…
在…下车 [zài…xià-chē] = to get off a vehicle at…
在…换乘 [zài…huàn-chéng] = to transfer to another vehicle at…

Sample Sentences B 🔊

第一，坐地铁3号线。[dì-yī, zuò dì-tiě sān hào xiàn]
First, take subway line 3.

第二，坐5路公交车。[dì-èr, zuò wǔ lù gōng-jiāo-chē]
Second, take No. 5 bus.

第三，要坐地铁9号线。[dì-sān, yào zuò dì-tié* jiǔ hào xiàn]
Third, (you) have to take subway line 9.

铁 (tiě) becomes tié when followed by a third tone syllable

第四，你要坐地铁10号线。[dì-sì, nǐ yào zuò dì-tiě shí hào xiàn]
Fourth, you have to take subway line 10.

我要坐地铁5号线吗？[wǒ yào zuò dì-tié wǔ hào xiàn ma?]
Do I have to take subway line 5?

然后，你要换乘地铁10号线。[rán-hòu, nǐ yào huàn-chéng dì-tiě shí hào xiàn]
Then, you have to transfer to subway line 10.

然后，你要在东四换乘地铁6号线。[rán-hòu, nǐ yào zài dōng-sì huàn-chéng dì-tiě liù hào xiàn]
Then, you have to transfer to subway line 6 at Dongsi.

最后，你在奥林匹克公园下车。[zuì-hòu, nǐ zài ào-lín-pǐ-kè gōng-yuán xià-chē]
Finally, you get off at Olympic Park.

Vocabulary C 🔊

会 [huì] = to know (a skill)

认识 [rèn-shí] = to know (a person)

知道 [zhī-dào] = to know (information)

能 [néng] = able to

Sample Sentences C 🔊

你会中文吗？[nǐ huì zhōng-wén ma?]
Do you know Chinese?

你认识萍萍吗？[nǐ rèn-shí píng-píng ma?]
Do you know Ping Ping?

你知道怎么去雍和宫吗？ [nǐ zhī-dào zěn-me qù yōng-hé-gōng ma?]
Do you know how to go to Yonghegong Lama Temple?

地铁6号线能去雍和宫吗？ [dì-tiě liù hào xiàn néng qù yōng-hé-gōng ma?]
Can the subway line 6 get to Yonghegong Lama Temple?

你知道地铁6号线能去雍和宫吗？ [nǐ zhī-dào dì-tiě liù hào xiàn néng qù yōng-hé-gōng ma?]
Do you know if subway line 6 can get to Yonghegong Lama Temple?

Sentence Structure Takeaway

If you would like to negate a verb, simply put 不 [bù] before a verb, for example:

不会 [bú huì] = to not know (a skill)

不认识 [bú rèn-shí] = to not know (a person)

不知道 [bù zhī-dào] = to not know (information)

不能 [bù néng] = unable to; can't

However, there is an exception to this form of negation, which you will learn in the next chapter.

> **Note**
>
> Did you notice that the character 不 appeared in second tone (bú) in "不会 (bú huì)" and "不认识 (bú rèn-shí)" while in fourth tone in "不知道 (bù zhī-dào)" and "不能 (bù néng)?" That is because pronunciation of the character 不 (bù) becomes second tone when followed by a fourth tone syllable. In summary, 一 [yī] and 不 [bù] are the two characters in Chinese whose tone changes to 2nd and 4th based on the tone of the following syllable.

我不会中文。[wǒ bú huì zhōng-wén]
I don't know Chinese.

我不认识萍萍。[wǒ bú rèn-shí píng-píng]
I don't know Ping Ping.

我不知道怎么去雍和宫。[wǒ bù zhī-dào zěn-me qù yōng-hé-gōng]
I don't know how to go to Yonghegong Lama Temple.

6号线不能去雍和宫。[liù hào xiàn bù néng qù yōng-hé-gōng]
Subway line 6 can't get to Yonghegong Lama Temple.

Recognizing Chinese Characters

1. 上 [shàng] = up
2. 下 [xià] = down
3. 不 [bù] = no; not

Did you notice that the character "上 (shàng)" is pointing upward and "下 (xià)" is pointing downward? The beauty of written Chinese is that many characters represent the universal forms in nature, and in this case, both characters "up 上 (shàng)" and "down 下 (xià)" are categorized as self-explanatory characters.

Sample Conversation

An An: 你好, 请问怎么去故宫？ [ní-hǎo, qǐng-wèn zěn-me qù gù-gōng?]
Hi, how do you go to the Forbidden City, please?

Beijinger: 第一，你要坐地铁5号线。[dì-yī, nǐ yào zuò dì-tié wǔ hào xiàn]
First, you have to take subway line 5.

然后，在东单换乘地铁1号线。[rán-hòu, zài dōng-dān huàn-chéng dì-tiě yī hào xiàn]
Then, you transfer to subway line 1 at Dongdan.

最后，你在天安门东下车。[zuì-hòu, nǐ zài tiān-ān-mén dōng xià-chē]
Finally, you get off at Tiananmen East.

An An: 地铁5号线能去天安门东吗？[dì-tié wǔ hào xiàn néng qù tiān-ān-mén dōng ma?]
Can subway line 5 get to Tiananmen East?

Beijinger: 不能，你要换乘。[bù néng, nǐ yào huàn-chéng]
No you can't, you have to transfer.

An An: 好的，谢谢。[hǎo de, xiè-xiè]
Okay, thank you.

Cultural Insights | Riding public transportation in Beijing

As in many other major cities in the world, the Beijing subway is rapid and crowded. Most lines operate between 5 a.m. and 11 p.m. The fare price is based on the distance that you travel. A trip is usually between ￥3 and ￥6, but can be higher if you travel further. In the busy streets of Beijing and during rush hours at subway stations, you may see volunteers who usually wear a red armband that says "志愿者 (zhì-yuàn-zhě)." They are there to maintain public order.

When riding the subway, instead of saying "excuse me" such as "不好意思 (bù-hǎo-yì-sī)" or "麻烦借过 (má-fán jiè-guò)," it is not surprising to hear people say "下车吗 (xià-chē ma) are you getting off the car" as an indicator that you are in their way of getting off. You can interpret it as "I would like to get off."

> Is it rude to say "下车吗 (xià-chē ma) are you getting off" instead of "excuse me?"

Everyone has his or her own perspective, and that is where cultural misunderstanding may arise. The reason that a person would ask "下车吗 (xià-chē ma)" is because they have to consider whether you are getting off the subway or not. If you intend to get off at the same station, saying "excuse me" doesn't really make a difference because the other person needs to get off also anyway. Therefore, saying "下车吗 (xià-chē ma) are you getting off the car" avoids bothering others when it's not necessary. This expression may not be used in cities other than Beijing, so you can always just say "不好意思 (bù-hǎo-yì-sī)" or "麻烦借过 (má-fán jiè-guò)" as "excuse me" if you are traveling in other cities in China.

Chapter 5 Exercise

1. What character do you add before a cardinal number (e.g. one) to make it into an ordinal number (e.g. first)?

   ....

2. What is the verb "to go to…" in Mandarin?

   ....

3. What do you add before a verb or adjective to negate?

   ....

4. Translate the following transitional words:

   然后 [rán-hòu]..

   最后 [zuì-hòu]..

5. Fill in the blanks.

   [zuò .... gōng-jiāo-chē]
   坐3路公交车。
   Take road 3 bus.

   [zuò ....]
   坐地铁7号线。
   Take subway line 7.

[..... ....]
你要坐地铁2号线。
You have to take subway line 2.

Chapter 6
How much is...?
…多少钱?

At 6 p.m., I arrived at the Forbidden City for an evening visit. The Forbidden City is a palace where 24 Chinese emperors from the Ming Dynasty to the end of the Qing Dynasty were based, and is located in the heart of Beijing. In this chapter, I will be getting my admission ticket to enter the Forbidden City. After reading this chapter, you will learn more about Chinese classifiers, higher digit numbers, and how to purchase a ticket with a discount based on your age or student status.

A beginner's guide to mastering conversational Mandarin Chinese

Notice in this chapter I am visiting the Forbidden City at 6 p.m. to complement the storyline; however, in reality, the latest time to enter the Forbidden City is between 3:40 and 4:10 p.m., and all exhibitions close between 4:30 and 5 p.m. This is to help preserve the palaces and because a lighting system to illuminate all the palaces would be extremely costly.

元 [yuán] is the Chinese currency, which is also known as Renminbi (RMB ￥).

Although the value of currencies fluctuates, 1元 [yuán] is approximately equivalent to $0.14, or 1 USD is approximately equivalent to ￥7.

However, in everyday life, people generally say 块 [kuài] to replace 元 [yuán]. For example:

1块 [yí kuài] = ￥1

5块 [wǔ kuài] = ￥5

10块 [shí kuài] = ￥10

> Like we learned before in Chapter 4, when you are using "2 (èr)" alone before a unit or classifier, it becomes 两 (liǎng). So ￥2 will be 两块 (liǎng kuài).

Let's explore how currency numbers are used in practical situations with generic terms and personal pronouns.

Vocabulary A 🔊

这些 [zhè-xiē] = these

那些 [nà-xiē] = those

东西 [dōng-xi] = thing

这些东西 [zhè-xiē dōng-xi] = these things

那些东西 [nà-xiē dōng-xi] = those things

我们 [wǒ-men] = we; us

你们 [nǐ-men] = you (plural)

他们/她们/它们 [tā-men] = they; them

Sample Sentences A 🔊

牛肉饭6块。[niú-ròu fàn liù kuài]
Beef with rice is ¥6.

海鲜面7块。[hǎi-xiān miàn qī kuài]
Seafood noodles are ¥7.

鸡肉拉面10块。[jī-ròu lā-miàn shí kuài]
Chicken ramen is ¥10.

这些8块。[zhè-xiē bā kuài]
These are ¥8.

Tip:

If you live outside of China where RMB is not the official currency, you can always just use 块 *(kuài) to indicate the basic unit of a local currency, such as "dollar" or "buck" in the U.S.*

Remember how in Chapter 2 we learned to order/request food from the flight attendant? In this chapter, we will incorporate the same sentence structure into purchasing an admission ticket, or anything else.

我想要… [wó xiǎng yào…] = I would like…

Vocabulary B 🔊

票 [piào] = ticket

门票 [mén-piào] = admission ticket

张 [zhāng] = classifier for flat rectangular object

一张门票 [yì-zhāng mén-piào] = one admission ticket

普通 [pǔ-tōng] = general; common

普通票 [pǔ-tōng piào] = general ticket

> **Note**
>
> Note that Mandarin is also referred to as "普通话 (pǔ-tōng-huà)," the common language.

一张学生票 [yì-zhāng xué-shēng piào] = one student ticket

学生证 [xué-shēng zhèng] = student ID

老人 [lǎo-rén] = senior

一张老人票 [yì-zhāng lǎo-rén piào] = one senior ticket

老人证 [lǎo-rén zhèng] = senior ID

Sample Sentences B 🔊

我想要一张门票。[wó xiǎng yào yì-zhāng mén-piào]
I would like an admission ticket.

我想要两张门票。[wó xiǎng yào liǎng-zhāng mén-piào]
I would like two admission tickets.

我想要一张学生票。[wó xiǎng yào yì-zhāng xué-shēng piào]
I would like one student ticket.

我想要一张学生票和两张普通票。
[wó xiǎng yào yì-zhāng xué-shēng piào hé liǎng-zhāng pǔ-tōng piào]
I would like one student ticket and two general tickets.

这是我的学生证。[zhè shì wǒ de xué-shēng zhèng]
This is my student ID.

这是我的。[zhè shì wǒ de]
This is mine.

Grammar Takeaway: This is the first time we have introduced the possessive modifier 的 (de) in this book. In general, adding 的 (de) at the end of a noun is similar to "…'s" in English. For example:

> Jessica的 [Jessica de] = Jessica's
>
> 我的 [wǒ de] = my; mine

A beginner's guide to mastering conversational Mandarin Chinese

你的 [nǐ de] = your(s)

他/她/它的 [tā de] = his/her(s)/its

老师的 [lǎo-shī de] = the teacher's

学生的 [xué-shēng de] = the student's

Now that we have requested an admission ticket, let's learn how to ask for the price.

多少 [duō-shǎo] = how many; how much
钱 [qián] = money
多少钱 [duō-shǎo qián] = how much (money)
一共 [yí-gòng] = total

一共 [yí-gòng] + 多少钱 [duō-shǎo qián]? = How much is it in total?

Vocabulary C 🔊

> Here are more examples of numbers higher than 10:

¥10 [shí] + ¥1 [yī] = ¥11 [shí-yī] = 11块 [shí-yī kuài]

¥10 [shí] + ¥4 [sì] = ¥14 [shí-sì] = 14块 [shí-sì kuài]

¥2 [èr] x ¥10 [shí] = ¥20 [èr-shí] = 20块 [èr-shí kuài]

¥2 [èr] x ¥10 [shí] + ¥6 [liù] = ¥26 [èr-shí-liù] = 26块 [èr-shí-liù kuài]

¥7 [qī] x ¥10 [shí] + ¥7 [qī] = ¥77 [qī-shí-qī] = 77块 [qī-shí-qī kuài]

100 = 一百 [yì-bǎi]

¥100 [yì-bǎi] = 一百块 [yì-bǎi kuài]

¥100 [yì-bǎi] + ¥40 [sì-shí] = ¥140 [yì-bǎi-sì-shí] = 140块 [yì-bǎi-sì-shí kuài]

¥100 [yì-bǎi] + ¥40 [sì-shí] + ¥9 [jiǔ] = ¥149 [yì-bǎi-sì-shí-jiǔ] = 149块 [yì-bǎi-sì-shí-jiǔ kuài]

Sample Sentences C 🔊

一共多少钱? [yí-gòng duō-shǎo qián?]
How much is it in total?

这个多少钱? [zhè-gè duō-shǎo qián?]
How much is this?

这些多少钱? [zhè-xiē duō-shǎo qián?]
How much are these?

这些一共多少钱? [zhè-xiē yí-gòng duō-shǎo qián?]
How much are these in total?

你的多少钱? [nǐ de duō-shǎo qián?]
How much is yours?

这个29块。 [zhè-gè èr-shí-jiǔ kuài]
This is ¥29.

一共92块。[yí-gòng jiǔ-shí-èr kuài]
It's ￥92 in total.

这些一共67块。[zhè-xiē yí-gòng liù-shí-qī kuài]
These are ￥67 in total.

那些67块。[nà-xiē liù-shí-qī kuài]
Those are ￥67.

Recognizing Chinese Characters

1. 多 [duō] = many; much; more
2. 少 [shǎo] = few; little
3. 钱 [qián] = money

Sample Conversation

Ticket Seller: 您好。[nín-hǎo]
Hello.

An An: 您好, 我想要两张门票。[nín-hǎo, wó xiǎng yào liǎng-zhāng mén-piào]
Hi, I would like two admission tickets.

一张普通票和一张学生票。[yì-zhāng pǔ-tōng piào hé yì-zhāng xué-shēng piào]
One general ticket and one student ticket.

	她是学生。[tā shì xué-shēng] She is a student.
Ticket Seller:	你有学生证吗? [ní yǒu xué-shēng zhèng ma?] Do you have a student ID?
Ping Ping:	这是我的学生证。[zhè shì wǒ de xué-shēng zhèng] This is my student ID.
An An:	一共多少钱? [yí-gòng duō-shǎo qián?] How much is it in total?
Ticket Seller:	学生票20块, 普通票60块。[xué-shēng piào èr-shí kuài, pǔ-tōng piào liù-shí kuài] The student ticket is ￥20, (and) the general ticket is ￥60. 一共80块。[yí-gòng bā-shí kuài] It's ￥80 in total.

Cultural Insights | Bargaining in China

Bargaining is not appropriate everywhere in China, for example, in chain stores and supermarkets. However, it is acceptable in most family-owned stores and in markets. Bargaining is a survival skill in China. Think of it as one of the beauties of experiencing a different culture, and also a chance for you to practice your Chinese with locals. Plus, you will find very good deals!

What can you bargain for?

- cars
- clothes
- furniture
- groceries in the market
- electronics

How do you bargain the price of a jacket listed as ￥80?

- After you learn about the price, give a price that is lower than what you expect to pay. For example, depending on the quality of the jacket, if you would like to get it for ￥60, ask for ￥50.
- Mention the flaws of the jacket that you can see, for example, if it's not warm enough for winters in Beijing, or the color of the jacket is very hard to match with other clothes.
- After bargaining back and forth and the lowest price offered is ￥65 and you are still not satisfied, try leaving the store as this jacket is really just another addition to your closet full of other treasures (it probably is!)

- But note that if this is something that you think is the deal of a lifetime, take it for ￥65 and know that you already used your opportunity to practice Chinese and also got a ￥15 discount.

Chapter 6 Exercise

1. What is the generic word for "thing" in Mandarin?

   ....

2. What is the possessive indicator in Mandarin that is similar to "…'s" in English?

   ....

3. How do you ask "how much is it in total?"

   ....

4. Translate the following sentences:

   [wó xiǎng yào yì-zhāng mén-piào]

   我想要一张门票。

   ....

   [xué-shēng piào shí-èr kuài]

   学生票12块。

   ....

[zhè shì wǒ de xué-shēng zhèng]

这是我的学生证。

....

5. Do you know how to say the following in Mandarin?

　　¥ 6 ....

　　¥ 16 ....

　　¥ 61 ....

Part II Review

- To express a skill/knowledge that you have, you can say. "我会… (wǒ huì…) I know…"
- To tell someone that you know some information, you can say. "我知道… (wǒ zhī-dào…) I know…"
- 在 (zài) is a preposition that is often used in Chinese. "在… (zài…)" means "at…"
- To turn a statement into a yes/no question, you add "吗 (ma)" at the end of the sentence.
- To get directions, you can ask "怎么去… (zěn-me qù…) how to get to…?"
- To tell someone to get on/off at a certain station, you can say "在…上车 (zài…shàng-chē) get on at…" or "在…下车 (zài…xià-chē) get off at…."
- To turn a cardinal number into an ordinal number, you add "第 (dì)" before the number.
- The verb for riding public transportation is "坐 (zuò) to ride."
- To ask how much something is, you can say "…多少钱 (…duō-shǎo qián) how much is…?"
- The generic noun for "thing" is 东西 (dōng-xi).
- Adding "不 (bù)" before a verb negates the sentence.
- …dollars = …块 (kuài)

Sample Paragraph

我想去天安门。我不知道怎么去。玛丽说, 第一, 我要坐地铁5号线。然后, 我要换乘地铁1号线, 在天安门东下车。

[wó xiǎng qù tiān-ān-mén。wǒ bù zhī-dào zěn-me qù。mǎ-lì shuō, dì-yī, wǒ yào zuò dì-tié wǔ hào xiàn。rán-hòu, wǒ yào huàn-chéng dì-tiě yī hào xiàn, zài tiān-ān-mén dōng xià-chē]

I want to go to Tiananmen. I don't know how to get there. Mary says that first, I have to take subway line 5. Then I have to transfer to subway line 1, (and) get off the subway at Tiananmen East.

Sample Exercise

Translate the following sentences.

1. How much are the beef noodles? […… …… …… …… …… ……?]
2. How much are your beef noodles? [….. …… …… …… …… …… …… ……?]
3. I don't know Chinese. [….. …… …… …… ……。]

Chapter 7
On Sundays I like to…
我星期天喜欢…

At 7 p.m., Ping Ping and I both got very hungry after touring the Forbidden City, and we decided to go to a Peking Duck restaurant nearby to have dinner. Peking Duck is an imperial dish that originated in Beijing. Slices of duck are usually wrapped in a lotus leaf (shaped) bun and eaten with scallions and plum sauce for dipping. At the restaurant, Ping Ping and I talked about what we like to do during weekends. After reading this chapter, you will be able to describe your hobbies in Mandarin along with the different days of the week.

Now, let's take a look at how we can use the basic numbers that we learned from Chapter 4 to change them into days of the week.

星期 [xīng-qī] = week

星期 [xīng-qī] + 一 [yī] = Monday

In Chinese, Monday is considered the first day of the week.

学 [xué] = to learn

中文 [zhōng-wén] = Chinese (language)

Subject + Time + Verb phrase

我 [wǒ] + 星期一 [xīng-qī-yī] + 学 [xué] + 中文 [zhōng-wén] = I learn Chinese on Monday

> *Tip:*
> Remember we learned in Chapter 1 that 学生 (xué-shēng) means "student?" That is because 学 (xué) means to learn, and 生 (shēng) means an apprentice. Together 学 (xué) + 生 (shēng) becomes a student, a learning apprentice.

Vocabulary A 🔊

星期一 [xīng-qī-yī] = Monday

星期二 [xīng-qī-èr] = Tuesday

星期三 [xīng-qī-sān] = Wednesday

星期四 [xīng-qī-sì] = Thursday

星期五 [xīng-qī-wǔ] = Friday

星期六 [xīng-qī-liù] = Saturday

星期天 [xīng-qī-tiān] = Sunday

周末 [zhōu-mò] = weekend

去上班 [qù shàng-bān] = to go to work

Sample Sentence A 🔊

我星期二学中文。[wǒ xīng-qī-èr xué zhōng-wén]
I learn Chinese on Tuesdays.

我星期二和星期三学中文。[wǒ xīng-qī-èr hé xīng-qī-sān xué zhōng-wén]
I learn Chinese on Tuesdays and Wednesdays.

我星期六去上班。[wǒ xīng-qī-liù qù shàng-bān]
I go to work on Saturdays.

我星期天不去上班。[wǒ xīng-qī-tiān bú qù shàng-bān]
I don't go to work on Sundays.

我星期四不学中文。[wǒ xīng-qī-sì bù xué zhōng-wén]
I don't learn Chinese on Thursdays.

> Remember, the tone change rule of 不 (bù) is applied when you switch tones. When the following character has the fourth tone, you use 不 (bú). Otherwise, you will use 不 (bù).

To recap, as we learned from Chapter 5, placing 不 (bù) before a verb negates the sentence, much like adding "not" in a sentence in English.

Now, let's take a look at how we can ask someone what he/she does on the weekends. Don't worry if you can't remember the sentence structure; you will be seeing more examples of the S.V.O., subject-verb-object structure in this chapter. For an interrogative sentence, we incorporate the S.V.O. sentence structure and make it S.V.Q., subject-verb-question. Let's take a look at an example:

做 [zuò] = to do

Subject + Time (adverb phrase) + Question phrase
你 [nǐ] + 周末 [zhōu-mò] + 做什么 [zuò shén-me] ? = What do you do on weekends?

Now, let's learn about more words for activities in order to answer the question by telling someone about your hobbies.

Vocabulary B 🔊

运动 [yùn-dòng] = to exercise

休息 [xiū-xi] = to rest

喜欢 [xǐ-huān] = to like

吃 [chī] = to eat

吃东西 [chī dōng-xi] = to eat (food)

菜 [cài] = dish; vegetable

吃中国菜 [chī zhōng-guó cài] = to eat Chinese cuisine

吃美国菜 [chī měi-guó cài] = to eat American cuisine

吃西班牙菜 [chī xī-bān-yá cài] = to eat Spanish cuisine

看 [kàn] = to look; to watch; to see

看书 [kàn-shū] = to read books

读书 [dú-shū] = to read books (out loud)

Although both 看书 (kàn-shū) and 读书 (dú-shū) mean "to read books," and 看书 (kàn-shū) literally means "to look at books" while 读书 (dú-shū) means "to read books out loud." In English reading books implies reading silently, but Chinese people differentiate clearly between reading silently and reading out loud. In English, we add "silently" and "out loud" after the verb "reading" to distinguish the difference between the two. However, in Chinese there are two distinct words, 看书 (kàn-shū) and 读书 (dú-shū).

When something is read silently, Chinese people say "看书 (kàn-shū) to look at books". When something is read out loud, they say "读书 (dú-shū)." In addition to this definition of "读书 (dú-shū)", "你在哪里读书 (nǐ zài ná-lǐ dú-shū)" is also a common expression for "where do you study?" But as you can see, this expression literally translates to "where do you read books?"

Sample Sentences B

你周末喜欢做什么? [nǐ zhōu-mò xǐ-huān zuò shén-me?]
What do you like to do on weekends?

我喜欢运动。[wó xǐ-huān yùn-dòng]
I like to exercise.

我星期天喜欢运动。[wǒ xīng-qī-tiān xǐ-huān yùn-dòng]
I like to exercise on Sundays.

我星期六休息。[wǒ xīng-qī-liù xiū-xi]
I am off on Saturdays. / I rest on Saturdays.

我喜欢吃中国菜。[wó xǐ-huān chī zhōng-guó cài]
I like to eat Chinese food.

我很喜欢吃西班牙菜。[wǒ hén xǐ-huān chī xī-bān-yá cài]
I really like to eat Spanish food.

我很喜欢看书。[wǒ hén xǐ-huān kàn-shū]
I really like to read books.

Remember in Chapter 5 we learned 上 (shàng) and 下 (xià) as "up" and "down?" In this chapter, we will use them with the generic classifier 个 (gè) to make your sentences more precise. Let's take a look at the examples below:

Vocabulary C

上个 [shàng-gè] = previous one

下个 [xià-gè] = next one

这个 [zhè-gè] = this one

那个 [nà-gè] = that one

这个星期天 [zhè-gè xīng-qī-tiān] = this Sunday

那个星期天 [nà-gè xīng-qī-tiān] = that Sunday

哪个 [nǎ-gè] = which one
哪个星期天 [nǎ-gè xīng-qī-tiān] = which Sunday

> In colloquial Mandarin you may also hear people say "nèi-gè" instead of "nà-gè" for "that" or simply as a filler word. It's similar to "ummm" in English.

Sample Sentences C

A: 你下个星期学中文吗? [nǐ xià-gè xīng-qī xué zhōng-wén ma?]
Are you going to learn Chinese next week?

B: 不学。[bù xué]
No. (not learning)

A: 你喜欢看书吗? [ní xǐ-huān kàn-shū ma?]
Do you like reading books?

B: 不喜欢。[bù xǐ-huān]
No. (don't like)

A: 你喜欢我吗? [ní xǐ-huān wǒ ma?]
Do you like me?

B: 不喜欢。[bù xǐ-huān]
No. (don't like)

A: 你下个周末去长城吗? [nǐ xià-gè zhōu-mò qù cháng-chéng ma?]
Are you going to the Great Wall next weekend?

B: 不去。[bú qù]
No. (not going)

A: 这个星期五我们吃中国菜吗? [zhè-gè xīng-qī-wú* wǒ-men chī zhōng-guó cài ma?]
Are we eating Chinese food this Friday?

> 五 (wǔ) becomes wú when followed by a third tone syllable

B: 不吃。[bù chī]
No. (not eating)

A: 这个星期五我们吃中国菜，好吗? [zhè-gè xīng-qī-wú wǒ-men chī zhōng-guó cài, hǎo-ma?]
(Let's) eat Chinese food this Friday. Is that good?

B: 不好。[bù hǎo]
No. (not good)

As you can see, to answer "no" in a yes-or-no question, you can't only say "不 (bù)." Instead, you add the main verb after "不 (bù)" to make the expression more natural and the answer more specific in Chinese.

Recognizing Chinese Characters

1. 中 [zhōng] = center; middle; medium
2. 国 [guó] = country
3. 书 [shū] = book

Sample Conversation

Ping Ping: 安安，你想吃什么？[ān-ān, ní xiǎng chī shén-me?]
An An, what do you want to eat?

An An: 我想吃北京烤鸭。你呢？[wó xiǎng chī běi-jīng kǎo-yā。ní-ne?]
I want to eat Peking Duck, what about you?

Ping Ping: 好啊，我喜欢吃北京烤鸭。[hǎo a, wó xǐ-huān chī běi-jīng kǎo-yā]
That's good, I like to eat Peking Duck.

An An: 萍萍，你周末喜欢做什么？[píng-píng, nǐ zhōu-mò xǐ-huān zuò shén-me?]
Ping Ping, what do you like to do on weekends?

Ping Ping: 我喜欢看书和运动。[wó xǐ-huān kàn-shū hé yùn-dòng]
I like to read and exercise.

An An: 你喜欢看什么书？[ní xǐ-huān kàn shén-me shū?]
What books do you like to read?

Ping Ping: 我喜欢看中文书。你周末喜欢做什么?
[wó xǐ-huān kàn zhōng-wén shū。nǐ zhōu-mò xǐ-huān zuò shén-me?]
I like to read Chinese books. What do you like to do on weekends?

An An: 我周末喜欢学中文。这个星期天你做什么?
[wǒ zhōu-mò xǐ-huān xué zhōng-wén。zhè-gè xīng-qī-tiān nǐ zuò shén-me?]
I like to learn Chinese on weekends. What are you doing this Sunday?

Ping Ping: 不知道。[bù zhī-dào]
I don't know.

An An: 我们去吃四川菜,好吗? [wǒ-men qù chī sì-chuān cài, hǎo-ma?]
Let's go eat Szechuan food. Is that good?

Ting: 好啊。[hǎo a]
That's good.

Cultural Insights | Expression of affection

Unlike in English where "love you" and "miss you" are often used between friends and families, or by couples, Chinese expressions for affections are very implicit and nonverbal. It is not surprising to hear children who were born and raised in China say that their parents never said "我爱你 (wǒ ài nǐ) I love you" to them, or vice versa. In addition to that, you will find it very rare for Chinese parents to ever praise their children at home even when they do exceptionally well in a certain area. However, that doesn't mean that they are not proud of their children. When parents want to express love for their children, they generally don't use words to express their feelings directly, but rather actions.

In the best-selling novel "The Joy Luck Club," little Waverly was embarrassed when her mother boasted to other parents about her winning a chess championship. Part of the reason is that traditional Chinese parenting can be very strict and demanding in the household, with not much warm and supportive praising. However, when compared to other parents, Waverly's mother was very proud of little Waverly for her achievements in playing chess.

Okay, then how do people express affection for someone in Chinese?

In early stages, you will catch people saying "我喜欢你 (wó xǐ-huān nǐ) I like you," "我很喜欢你 (wó hén xǐ-huān nǐ) I really like you," or even "我想跟你在一起 (wó xiǎng gēn nǐ zài yì-qǐ) I want to be with you" if used in a romantic relationship.

Chapter 7 Exercise

1. What do you add before numbers 1-6 to make it the corresponding day of the week?
   ....

2. What is the most basic Chinese sentence structure?
   ....

3. How do you ask someone what does he/she like to do?
   ....

4. Translate the following sentences:

   我喜欢中文。[wó xǐ-huān zhōng-wén]
   ....

   我不喜欢运动。[wǒ bù xǐ-huān yùn-dòng]
   ....

   我周末不喜欢去上班。[wǒ zhōu-mò bù xǐ-huān qù shàng-bān]
   ....

5. Fill in the blanks.

   A: 你喜欢什么? [ní .... shén-me?]
   What do you like?

A: 你喜欢吃什么? [ní .... shén-me?]
What do you like to eat?

Chapter 8
Family Members
家人

At 8 p.m., Ping Ping and I were still at the restaurant, and I pulled out a family photo from my wallet to show her everyone in my family. After reading this chapter, you will be able to refer to different members of your family and will also know how to ask and answer questions that relate to your family.

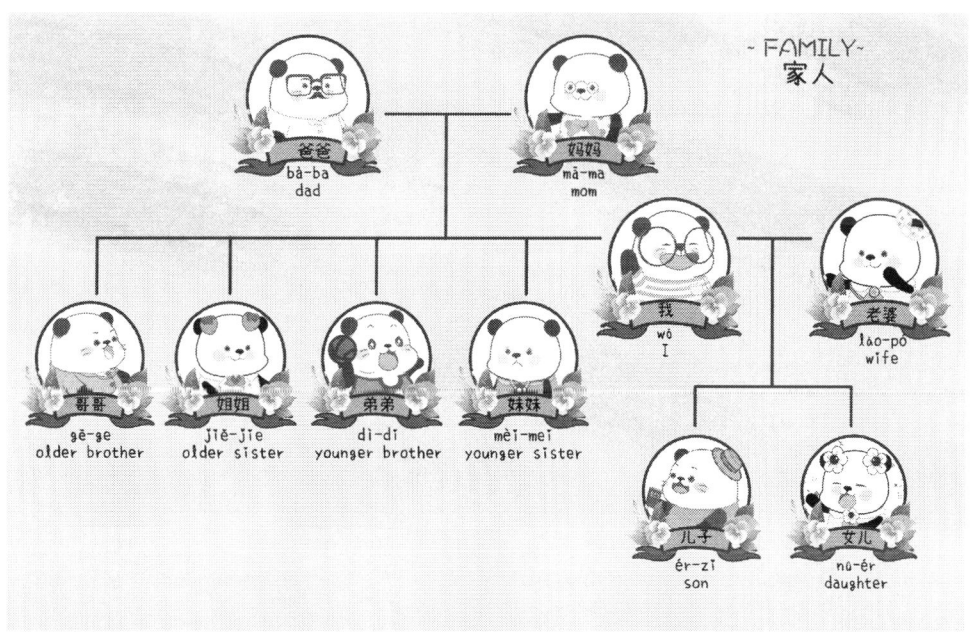

~ FAMILY ~
家人

爸爸	bà-ba	dad
妈妈	mā-ma	mom
我	wǒ	I
老婆	lǎo-po	wife
哥哥	gē-ge	older brother
姐姐	jiě-jie	older sister
弟弟	dì-di	younger brother
妹妹	mèi-mei	younger sister
儿子	ér-zi	son
女儿	nǚ-ér	daughter

We have used 的 (de) very often in Mandarin for many different purposes. In Chapter 4, I officially introduced one of the main usage of 的 (de). Let's review it again here.

…的 […de] …'s (possessive)
Susan + 的 [de] = Susan's
我 [wǒ] + 的 [de] = my

However, when you are talking about your family members or someone who is very close to you, you can omit 的 [de]. Take a look at the example below.

妈妈 [mā-ma] = mom
我 [wǒ] + 妈妈 [mā-ma] = my mom

Vocabulary A 🔊

Family Members

English	Formal	Informal/Other Names Used
mom	妈妈 (mā-ma)	妈 (mā)
dad	爸爸 (bà-ba)	爸 (bà)
older sister	姐姐 (jiě-jie)	姐 (jiě)
younger sister	妹妹 (mèi-mei)	妹 (mèi)
older brother	哥哥 (gē-ge)	哥 (gē)
younger brother	弟弟 (dì-di)	弟 (dì)

child(ren)	孩子 (hái-zi)	小孩 (xiǎo-hái)
daughter	女儿 (nǚ-ér)	-
son	儿子 (ér-zi)	-

Sample Sentences A 🔊

她是我妈妈。[tā shì wǒ mā-ma]
She is my mom.

这是我妈妈。[zhè shì wǒ mā-ma]
This is my mom.

那是我哥。[nà shì wǒ gē]
That is my older brother.

他是我爸爸。[tā shì wǒ bà-ba]
He is my dad.

我爸喜欢看书。[wǒ bà xǐ-huān kàn-shū]
My dad likes to read.

我妈喜欢吃美国菜。[wǒ mā xǐ-huān chī měi-guó cài]
My mom likes to eat American food.

As we learned in the last chapter, adding 不 (bù) negates the verb in a statement. There is one verb that is negated differently, "有 (yǒu) to have." Now we are going to take a look at how you actually negate 有 (yǒu).

有 [yǒu] = to have
没有 [méi-yǒu] = to not have

Vocabulary B 🔊

朋友 [péng-yǒu] = friend

男朋友 [nán péng-yǒu] = boyfriend

女朋友 [nǚ péng-yǒu] = girlfriend

老公 [lǎo-gōng] = husband

老婆 [lǎo-pó] = wife

很多 [hěn-duō] = many

Sample Sentences B 🔊

你有哥哥吗? [ní yǒu gē-ge ma?]
Do you have (an) older brother?

我有妹妹。[wó yǒu mèi-mei]
I have (a) younger sister.

我有一个妹妹。[wó yǒu yí-gè mèi-mei]
I have one younger sister.

我没有妹妹。[wǒ méi-yǒu mèi-mei]
I don't have a younger sister.

我有一个姐姐和一个弟弟。[wó yǒu yí-gè jiě-jie hé yí-gè dì-di]
I have an older sister and a younger brother.

你有女朋友吗?[ní yóu nǔ péng-yǒu ma?]
Do you have a girlfriend?

我有女朋友。[wó yóu nǔ péng-yǒu]
I have a girlfriend.

我有一个女朋友。[wó yǒu yí-gè nǔ péng-yǒu]
I have one girlfriend.

我没有很多女朋友。[wǒ méi-yóu hěn-duō nǔ péng-yǒu]
I don't have many girlfriends.

Vocabulary C 🔊

家 [jiā] = home; house; family

家人 [jiā-rén] = family member

谁 [shéi] = who

…是谁？ […shì shéi?] = Who is…?

Sample Sentences C 🔊

他是谁？[tā shì shéi?]
Who is he?

这是谁？[zhè shì shéi?]
Who is this?

哪个是你哥哥？[nǎ-gè shì nǐ gē-ge?]
Which one is your older brother?

你姐姐是谁？[ní jiě-jie shì shéi?]
Who is your older sister?

我不知道你姐姐是谁。[wǒ bù zhī-dào ní jiě-jie shì shéi]
I don't know who your older sister is.

你男朋友是谁？[nǐ nán péng-yǒu shì shéi?]
Who is your boyfriend?

哪个是你老公？[nǎ-gè shì ní lǎo-gōng?]
Which one is your husband?

Recognizing Chinese Characters

1. 女 [nǔ] = female; woman
2. 男 [nán] = male; man
3. 有 [yǒu] = to have

Sample Conversation

Ping Ping: 安安, 你有兄弟姐妹吗? [ān-ān, ní yǒu xiōng-dì-jiě-mèi ma?]
An An, do you have any siblings?

An An: 我有一个弟弟和一个妹妹。 [wó yǒu yí-gè dì-di hé yí-gè mèi-mei]
I have a younger brother and a younger sister.

Ping Ping: 你还有什么家人? [nǐ hái yǒu shén-me jiā-rén?]
What other family members do you have?

An An: 我有爸爸和妈妈。 [wó yǒu bà-ba hé mā-ma]
I have mom and dad (in my family).

Ping Ping: 你有照片吗? [ní yǒu zhào-piàn ma?]
Do you have pictures?

An An: 有。这个是我爸爸，这个是我妈妈，这个是我弟弟，这个是我妹妹。
[yǒu。zhè-gè shì wǒ bà-ba, zhè-gè shì wǒ mā-ma, zhè-gè shì wǒ dì-di, zhè-gè shì wǒ mèi-mei]
Yes, I have (one). This is my dad, this is my mom, this is my younger brother, and this is my younger sister.

Cultural Insights

Unlike English where you can simply use "brother" and "sister," "aunt" and "uncle," or simply "cousin" to indicate kinship, the Chinese culture is very particular about the closeness of kinship. For example, as we have learned, there are specific words that specify an older or younger brother or sister. There are specific titles for mom's older brother, mom's younger brother, dad's older brother, dad's younger sister, mom's older first cousin who's a female…the list goes on and on, and sometimes even a native speaker has trouble telling the difference between the titles of relatives. This is just for you to know, and there is no need to worry about knowing each one of them now.

> There are family calculator apps online that help you figure out how you can address your relatives.

Chapter 8 Exercise

1. Is it necessary to add the possessive modifier 的 (de) when you are referring to your family members?
   ....

2. Translate the following sentences:

   Who is she?
   ....

   Do you have a boyfriend?
   ....

   [nǎ-gè shì ní nǔ-péng-yǒu?]
   哪个是你女朋友?
   ....

   [ní nǔ-péng-yǒu shì shéi?]
   你女朋友是谁?
   ....

3. Fill in the blanks.
   [...... ...... liǎng-gè gē-ge]
   我有两个哥哥。
   I have two older brothers.

   [...... .... mèi-mei]
   我没有妹妹。
   I don't have a younger sister.

Chapter 9
My birthday is on...
我的生日是…

At 9 p.m., Ping Ping told me when her birthday would be and invited me to her birthday gathering later this month. After reading Chapter 9, you will be able to express dates by using cardinal numbers that we learned in Chapter 4 and tell someone your age. You will also learn about the culture of Chinese banquets.

Now, let's take a look at how to tell your age by using numbers that we learned:

岁 [suì] = year (of age)

number + 岁 [suì] = ... years old*

我 [wǒ] + 30 [sān-shí] + 岁 [suì] = I am 30 years old.

*Note that 岁 [suì] can only be used for people, animals, or other animated objects such as cartoon characters.

Vocabulary A

多少岁 [duō-shǎo suì] = how many years old

什么时候 [shén-me shí-hòu] = when

生日 [shēng-rì] = birthday

为什么 [wèi-shén-me] = why (lit. for what)

因为 [yīn-wèi] = because

Sample Sentences A 🔊

你多少岁? [nǐ duō-shǎo suì?]
How old are you?

你妹妹多少岁? [nǐ mèi-mei duō-shǎo suì?]
How old is your younger sister?

我哥哥29岁。[wǒ gē-ge èr-shí-jiǔ suì]
My older brother is 29 years old.

你什么时候生日? [nǐ shén-me shí-hòu shēng-rì?]
When is your birthday?

你老婆什么时候生日? [ní lǎo-pó shén-me shí-hòu shēng-rì?]
When is your wife's birthday?

你好朋友什么时候生日? [ní hǎo péng-yǒu shén-me shí-hòu shēng-rì?]
When is your good friend's birthday?

为什么你生日想吃美国菜? [wèi-shén-me nǐ shēng-rì xiǎng chī měi-guó cài?]
Why do you want to eat American food on your birthday?

因为我喜欢吃美国菜。[yīn-wèi wó xǐ-huān chī měi-guó cài]
Because I like to eat American food.

为什么你喜欢她? [wèi-shén-me ní xǐ-huān tā?]
Why do you like her?

不为什么。[bú wèi-shén-me]
Just because. (lit. no why.)

Now, let's take a look at how we can express dates in Chinese to answer the birthday questions from Sample Sentences A:

Vocabulary B 🔊

年 [nián] = year

月 [yuè] = month

日 [rì] / 号 [hào] = day (written vs. spoken)

2009年 [èr-líng-líng-jiǔ nián] = the year 2009

2018年 [èr-líng-yī*-bā nián] = the year 2018

*When 一 [yī] appears as a number in a date, the tone change rule doesn't apply

1月 [yī-yuè] = January

2月 [èr-yuè] = February

5月 [wǔ-yuè] = May

10月 [shí-yuè] = October

12月 [shí-èr-yuè] = December

> As you can see, adding 月 (yuè) after the number turns a number into its corresponding month.

15号 [shí-wǔ hào] = 15th; No. 15

21号 [èr-shí-yī hào] = 21st; No. 21

30号 [sān-shí hào] = 30th; No. 30

2009年4月21号 [èr-líng-líng-jiǔ nián sì-yuè èr-shí-yī hào] = Apr. 21, 2009

2017年12月18号 [èr-líng-yī-qī nián shí-èr-yuè shí-bā hào] = Dec. 18, 2017

Question: Why isn't the year placed at the end of the date?

This is due to a cross-cultural difference between China and the U.S. The Chinese culture considers everything in its whole entity, and therefore often emphasizes the big over the small. For example, when Chinese people talk about a date, they go from the year to the month, and then to the day. When they mention an address, they go from the state to the city, and from the street to the house number. As we learned how to address someone in Chapter 2, Chinese speakers also say the last name before first name. Just remember bigger units always come before smaller units.

Sample Sentences B

我的生日是4月2号。[wǒ de shēng-rì shì sì-yuè èr hào]
My birthday is on Apr. 2nd.

她的生日是8月17号。[tā de shēng-rì shì bā-yuè shí-qī hào]
Her birthday is on Aug. 17th.

我男朋友的生日是10月20号。[wǒ nán péng-yǒu de shēng-rì shì shí-yuè èr-shí hào]
My boyfriend's birthday is on Oct. 20th.

我不知道你什么时候生日。[wǒ bù zhī-dào nǐ shén-me shí-hòu shēng-rì]
I don't know when your birthday is.

你知道你好朋友什么时候生日吗?[nǐ zhī-dào ní hǎo péng-yǒu shén-me shí-hòu shēng-rì ma?]
Do you know when your good friend's birthday is?

我不知道。[wǒ bù zhī-dào]
I don't know.

我怎么知道?[wó zěn-me zhī-dào?]
How would I know?

Vocabulary C

今年 [jīn-nián] = this year
这个月 [zhè-gè yuè] = this month
天 [tiān] = day; sky
今天 [jīn-tiān] = today
昨天 [zuó-tiān] = yesterday
明天 [míng-tiān] = tomorrow

> Why can you say "今年 (jīn-nián) this year" and "今天 (jīn-tiān) today" but not "今月 (jīn-yuè)?" Some people claim that because "月 (yuè)" also means "moon," saying "今月 (jīn-yuè)" can be interpreted as "the present moon." Therefore adding the classifier 个 (gè) for "this month 这个月 (zhè-gè yuè)" is more clear.

A beginner's guide to mastering conversational Mandarin Chinese

Sample Sentences C 🔊

我今年53岁。[wǒ jīn-nián wǔ-shí-sān suì]
I am 53 (years old) this year.

今天是我的生日。[jīn-tiān shì wǒ de shēng-rì]
Today is my birthday.

昨天是我朋友的生日。[zuó-tiān shì wǒ péng-yǒu de shēng-rì]
Yesterday was my friend's birthday.

这个月是我的生日。[zhè-gè yuè shì wǒ de shēng-rì]
My birthday is this month.

今年是2018年。[jīn-nián shì èr-líng-yī-bā nián]
This year is 2018.

昨天是2018年8月8号。[zuó-tiān shì èr-líng-yī-bā nián bā-yuè bā hào]
Yesterday was Aug. 8th, 2018.

今年没有2月29号。[jīn-nián méi yǒu èr-yuè èr-shí-jiǔ hào]
There is no February 29th this year.

明天是我儿子的生日。[míng-tiān shì wǒ ér-zi de shēng-rì]
Tomorrow is my son's birthday.

2020年有2月29号。[èr-líng-èr-líng nián yǒu èr-yuè èr-shí-jiǔ hào]
There is a February 29th in 2020.

Actually, there are no verb tenses in Chinese. In the last two examples given, though the translation here is in the present, the sentences could also indicate the future or the past. Usually the correct interpretation can be understood from context.

Recognizing Chinese Characters

1. 年 [nián] = year
2. 月 [yuè] = month
3. 日 [rì] = day; sun

Sample Conversation

Ping Ping: 安安, 你什么时候生日? [ān-ān, nǐ shén-me shí-hòu shēng-rì?]
An An, when is your birthday?

An An: 我1月13号生日。你呢? [wǒ yī-yuè shí-sān hào shēng-rì。nǐ ne?]
My birthday is on January 13th. What about you?

Ping Ping: 我的生日是这个月18号, 下个星期六。
[wǒ de shēng-rì shì zhè-gè yuè shí-bā hào, xià-gè xīng-qī-liù]
My birthday is the 18th of this month, next Saturday.

An An: 真的吗? 你今年多少岁? [zhēn-de ma? nǐ jīn-nián duō-shǎo suì?]
Really? How old are you this year?

Ping Ping: 我20岁。下个星期六我们去吃中国菜吧!
[wǒ èr-shí suì。xià-gè xīng-qī-liù wǒ-men qù chī zhōng-guó cài ba!]
I am 20 years old (in human years). Let's have Chinese food next Saturday!

An An: 好, 去哪里吃啊? [hǎo, qù ná-lǐ chī a?]
That's good, where (do we) go to eat?

Ping Ping: 我们去东四吧! 我喜欢那里的北京烤鸭。
[wǒ-men qù dōng-sì ba! wó xǐ-huān nà-lǐ de běi-jīng kǎo-yā]
Let's go to Dongsi! I like the Peking Duck there.

An An: 太好了。[tài hǎo le]
That's great!

Cultural Insights

Traditional large Chinese banquets are generally held for weddings "喜酒 (xí-jiǔ)", a child's one-month old celebration "满月酒 (mǎn-yuè-jiǔ)" (similar to baby shower but happens after baby's birth), and an elderly person's 60th, 70th or 80th birthday "大寿 (dà-shòu)." The size of the banquet depends on the budget of the host, and the number of tables can range from as little as one table to hundreds of tables. One table usually can fit 10 to 12 people. In the U.S., friends and families usually support the hosts by giving wedding or baby gifts from registries. In a traditional Chinese banquet, it is very common for guests to give cash by putting it into a red envelope and handing it to the host while saying a couple of blessing words in Chinese.

Chapter 9 Exercise

1. What is the order in Chinese to say a date?

   ....

2. Can you use "岁 (suì)" to express the age of a building?

   ....

3. Translate the following Sentences:

   [nǐ de shēng-rì shì shén-me shí-hòu?]
   你的生日是什么时候?

   ....

   My birthday is on July 29th.

   ....

   [jīn-tiān shì èr-líng-yī-bā nián shí-yuè shí-yī hào]
   今天是2018年10月11号。

   ....

4. Fill in the blanks.

   [wǒ .... èr-shí-èr suì]
   我今年22岁。
   I am 22 this year.

[...... .... shì jiǔ-yuè]
这个月是9月。
This (month) is September.

Part III Review

- To specify the days of the week, you add "星期 (xīng-qī) week" before the cardinal number, except for Sunday.
- To tell someone what you like to do on weekends, you can say "我周末喜欢…(wǒ zhōu-mò xǐ-huān…) I like to…on the weekends."
- To emphasize that you really like something, you can say "很喜欢… (hén xǐ-huān…) like…very much."
- The previous one = 上个 (shàng-gè)
- The next one = 下个 (xià-gè)
- To answer a yes/no question, you need to explicitly state the verb. For example, to answer "yes" for the question "你喜欢吗 (ní xǐ-huān ma) do you like it," you say 喜欢 (xǐ-huān); to answer "no," you say "不喜欢 (bù xǐ-huān)."
- To tell someone your age, you can say "我…岁 (wǒ…suì)," adding your age between "wǒ" and "suì."
- Possessive form is: Pronoun + 的 (de) = …'s
- Month of the year = Number + 月 (yuè)
- Day of the month = Number + 号 (hào)
- 有 (yǒu) = to have; there is
- 没有 (méi-yǒu) = to not have; there isn't

Sample Paragraphs

我星期六要上班，星期天我喜欢看书。我很喜欢看西班牙语书，我不喜欢看英文书。
8月17号是我朋友的生日。我不知道她喜欢什么。她喜欢看书吗？她喜欢吃中国菜吗？我想给她买书。

[wǒ xīng-qī-liù yào shàng-bān, xīng-qī-tiān wó xǐ-huān kàn-shū。wǒ hén xǐ-huān kàn xī-bān-yá-yǔ shū, wǒ bù xǐ-huān kàn yīng-wén shū。
bā-yuè shí-qī hào shì wǒ péng-yǒu de shēng-rì。wǒ bù zhī-dào tā xǐ-huān shén-me。tā xǐ-huān kàn-shū ma? tā xǐ-huān chī zhōng-guó cài ma? wó xiáng gěi tā mǎi shū]

I have to go to work on Saturdays, (and) I like to read on Sundays. I really like to read Spanish books, (and) I don't like to read English books.

August 17th is my friend's birthday. I don't know what she likes. Does she like to read? Does she like to eat Chinese food? I want to buy books for her.

Sample Exercise

Translate the following sentences:

1. Do you like to read Chinese books on weekends?

   [...... ....?]

2. [wó méi-yǒu dì-di.]

   ....

3. [wǒ mèi-mei de shēng-rì shì sì-yuè èr-shí-jiǔ hào.]

   ....

Chapter 10
Journaling: past, present, and the future
写日记：过去、现在、将来

At 10 p.m., I returned to my Airbnb apartment in Beijing and wrote my journal entry for the day. I wrote about the past, present, and the future in my journal. After reading this journal entry, you will be able to use different participles to indicate whether an event happened in the past, present, or future.

In the last chapter, we learned that there are no tenses in Chinese, but rather what we call aspects. That means the verb form does not change, no matter when the event happens. However, there are aspect markers (similar to "...ing," "...ed" and "will" in English) that we can add before/after a verb to indicate whether the event happens in the past, present, or the future. Stating time aspects in Chinese is very straight forward. Let's take a look at the first example.

Simple Past

verb + 了 [le] = ...ed
吃 [chī] = to eat

吃了 [chī le] = ate

Vocabulary A

Verb	English	Verb with aspectual marker	English
喝 [hē]	to drink	喝了 [hē le]	drank
等 [děng]	to wait	等了 [děng le]	waited
买 [mǎi]	to buy	买了 [mǎi le]	bought
想 [xiǎng]	to think	想了 [xiǎng le]	thought
忘 [wàng]	to forget	忘了 [wàng le]	forgot

Sample Sentences A 🔊

我喝了一杯奶茶。[wǒ hē le yì-bēi nǎi-chá]
I drank a cup of milk tea.

我今天喝了很多。[wǒ jīn-tiān hē le hěn-duō]
I drank a lot (of alcohol) today.

我今天喝了很多咖啡。[wǒ jīn-tiān hē le hěn-duō kā-fēi]
I drank a lot of coffee today.

我等了一个星期。[wó děng le yí-gè xīng-qī]
I waited for a week.

我买了两张门票。[wó mǎi le liǎng-zhāng mén-piào]
I bought two tickets.

我买了很多东西。[wó mǎi le hěn-duō dōng-xi]
I bought a lot of things.

我想了一天。[wó xiǎng le yì-tiān]
I thought (about it) for a day.

我忘了。[wǒ wàng le]
I forgot.

我忘了今天是我哥哥的生日。[wǒ wàng le jīn-tiān shì wǒ gē-ge de shēng-rì]
I forgot that today is my older brother's birthday.

Present Progressive

在 [zài] + verb = ...ing

在吃 [zài chī] = eating

> Notice that this 在 (zài) is the same character as the one we used in Chapter 3 as a preposition to mark the location, e.g. 在哪里 (zài ná-lǐ).

Vocabulary B 🔊

Verb	English	Verb with aspectual marker	English
学 [xué]	to learn	在学 [zài xué]	learning
说 [shuō]	to say	在说 [zài shuō]	saying
听 [tīng]	to listen	在听 [zài tīng]	listening
做 [zuò]	to do; to make	在做 [zài zuò]	doing; making
看 [kàn]	to look; to watch; to read (silently)	在看 [zài kàn]	looking; watching; reading

Sample Sentences B 🔊

我在学中文。[wǒ zài xué zhōng-wén]
I am learning Chinese.

我在学很多东西。[wǒ zài xué hěn-duō dōng-xi]
I am learning a lot of things.

我在说，他的普通话很好。[wǒ zài shuō, tā-de pǔ-tōng-huà hén hǎo]
I am saying (that) his Mandarin is very good.

我在说你。[wǒ zài shuō nǐ]
I am talking about you.

我在听。[wǒ zài tīng]
I am listening.

我在听音乐。[wǒ zài tīng yīn-yuè]
I am listening to music.
音乐 [yīn-yuè] = music

你在做什么? [nǐ zài zuo shén-me?]
What are you doing?
做 [zuò] = to do

我在做中国菜。[wǒ zài zuò zhōng-guó cài]
I am making Chinese food.

我在看书。[wǒ zài kàn-shū]
I am reading (a) book.

我在看微信朋友圈。[wǒ zài kàn wēi-xìn péng-yǒu quān]
I am looking at Moments (lit. friend's circle) on WeChat.

Note that "是 (shì) is/am/are" is not used here before a verb.

Future

会 [huì] + verb = will…

会吃 [huì chī] = will eat

Vocabulary C 🔊

> 微信 (wēi-xìn), or WeChat, is the most popular messaging and social media app used in Mainland China. Moments, or 朋友圈 (péng-yǒu quān) in Chinese, is a function on WeChat that allows you to see updates from other friends.

Verb	English	Verb with aspectual marker	English
去 [qù]	to go	会去 [huì qù]	will go
帮 [bāng]	to help	会帮 [huì bāng]	will help
去上班 [qù shàng-bān]	to go to work	会去上班 [huì qù shàng-bān]	will go to work
坐 [zuò]	to sit; to ride	会坐 [huì zuò]	will sit; will ride
有 [yǒu]	to have	会有 [huì yǒu]	will have

A beginner's guide to mastering conversational Mandarin Chinese

Sample Sentences C 🔊

我会去香港。[wǒ huì qù xiāng-gǎng]
I will go to Hong Kong.

你会去北京吗?[nǐ huì qù běi-jīng ma?]
Will you go to Beijing?

我会帮你。[wǒ huì bāng nǐ]
I will help you.

我会帮他们做这个。[wǒ huì bāng tā-men zuò zhè-gè]
I will help them to do this.

明天是星期天,我不会去上班。[míng-tiān shì xīng-qī-tiān, wǒ bú huì qù shàng-bān]
Tomorrow is Sunday; I will not go to work.

我会坐地铁6号线。[wǒ huì zuò dì-tiě liù hào xiàn]
I will take subway line 6.

下个星期没有地铁6号线,我会坐地铁10号线去上班。
[xià-gè xīng-qī méi-yǒu dì-tiě liù hào xiàn, wǒ huì zuò dì-tiě shí hào xiàn qù shàng-bān]
There is no subway line 6 next week, (and) I will take subway line 10 to go to work.

我会有很多钱。[wǒ huì yóu hěn-duō qián]
I will have a lot of money.

我不会有很多女朋友。[wǒ bú huì yóu hěn-duō nǔ péng-yǒu]
I will not have many girlfriends.

Comparisons

Verb	...ed	...ing	will...
买 [mǎi] to buy	买了 [mǎi le]	在买 [zài mǎi]	会买 [huì mǎi]
说 [shuō] to say	说了 [shuō le]	在说 [zài shuō]	会说 [huì shuō]
去 [qù] to go	去了 [qù le]	在去 [zài qù]	会去 [huì qù]

Recognizing Chinese Characters

1. 在 [zài] = ...ing; at
2. 会 [huì] = will; to know (a skill)
3. 说 [shuō] = to say

Sample Diary 🔊

2018年8月10日　星期五
[èr-líng-yī-bā nián bā-yuè shí rì, xīng-qī-wǔ]
August 10th, 2018 Friday

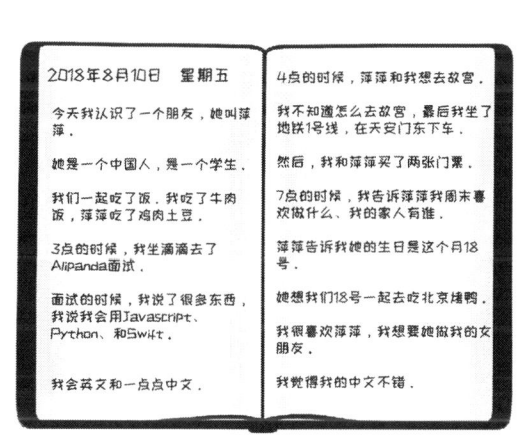

A beginner's guide to mastering conversational Mandarin Chinese

今天我认识了一个朋友,她叫萍萍。
[jīn-tiān wǒ rèn-shí le yí-gè péng-yǒu, tā jiào píng-píng]
Today I met a friend, her name is Ping Ping.

她是一个中国人,是一个学生。
[tā shì yí-gè zhōng-guó rén, shì yí-gè xué-shēng]
She is Chinese, (and) she's a student.

我们一起吃了饭。我吃了牛肉饭,萍萍吃了鸡肉土豆。
[wǒ-men yì-qǐ chī le fàn. wǒ chī le niú-ròu fàn, píng-píng chī le jī-ròu tǔ-dòu]
We ate together. I ate beef with rice, (and) Ping Ping ate chicken (with mashed) potatoes.

3点的时候,我坐滴滴去了Alipanda面试。[sān-diǎn de shí-hòu, wǒ zuò dī-dī qù le Alipanda miàn-shì]
At 3 o'clock, I took a Didi to go to Alipanda for an interview.
面试 [miàn-shì] = interview

面试的时候,我说了很多东西,我说我会用Javascript、Python、和Swift。
[miàn-shì de shí-hòu, wǒ shuō le hěn-duō dōng-xi, wǒ shuō wǒ huì yòng Javascript、Python、hé Swift]
During the interview, I said many things, I said I know how to use Javascript, Python, and Swift.

我会英文和一点点中文。[wǒ huì yīng-wén hé yì-diǎn-diǎn zhōng-wén]
I know English and a little Chinese.

4点的时候,萍萍和我想去故宫。[sì-diǎn de shí-hòu, píng-píng hé wó xiǎng qù gù-gōng]
At 4 o'clock, Ping Ping and I would like to go to the Forbidden City.

我不知道怎么去故宫，最后我坐了地铁1号线，在天安门东下车。
[wǒ bù zhī-dào zěn-me qù gù-gōng, zuì-hòu wǒ zuò le dì-tiě yī hào xiàn, zài tiān-ān-mén dōng xià-chē]
I didn't know how to go to the Forbidden City; eventually I took subway line 1, and got off at Tiananmen East.

然后，我和萍萍买了两张门票。
[rán-hòu, wǒ hé píng-píng mǎi le liǎng-zhāng mén-piào]
Then, Ping Ping and I bought two admission tickets.

7点的时候，我告诉萍萍我周末喜欢做什么、我的家人有谁。
[qī-diǎn de shí-hòu, wǒ gào-sù píng-píng wǒ zhōu-mò xǐ-huān zuò shén-me, wǒ-de jiā-rén yǒu shéi]
At 7 o'clock, I told Ping Ping what I like to do on weekends, (and) whom I have in my family.
告诉 [gào-sù] = to tell

萍萍告诉我她的生日是这个月18号。[píng-píng gào-sù wǒ tā de shēng-rì shì zhè-gè yuè shí-bā hào]
Ping Ping told me her birthday is the 18th of this month.

她想我们18号一起去吃北京烤鸭。
[tā xiáng* wǒ-men shí-bā hào yì-qǐ qù chī běi-jīng kǎo-yā]
She would like us to go eat Peking Duck together on the 18th.

想 (xiǎng) becomes xiáng when followed by a third tone syllable

我很喜欢萍萍，我想要她做我的女朋友。
[wǒ hén xǐ-huān píng-píng, wǒ xiǎng-yào tā zuò wǒ-de nǚ péng-yǒu]
I really like Ping Ping, (and) I would like her to be my girlfriend.

我觉得我的中文不错。[wǒ jué-dé wǒ-de zhōng-wén bú cuò]
I think my Chinese is not bad.
不错 [bú cuò] = not bad

Cultural Insights | What you should expect

When traveling in China, you should expect to see/use squat toilets at private/public bathrooms, including local homes and businesses.

Why squat toilets?
Many claim that the cost is much lower to maintain the cleanliness of squat toilets than of flush toilets. In addition to the cost, the population in China is at the world's highest, and public bathrooms cannot be cleaned as frequently as in other places. So make sure to always bring tissues with you because many public facilities don't offer toilet paper.

When it is your first time visiting a Chinese family's apartment, or even your host family's apartment, always ask if you should take off your shoes and switch to a pair of slippers. It is a Chinese custom to remove shoes at the door. Even if the host says no, it doesn't hurt to ask and to show politeness. Wearing slippers helps to keep both the bathroom and your feet clean when the host family has a squat toilet at home.

Chapter 10 Exercise

1. Does Chinese have tenses?
   ....

2. Which aspectual marker do you need after a verb to indicate an event happened in the past?
   ....

3. Which aspectual marker do you need before a verb to indicate an event is happening now?
   ....

4. Which aspectual marker do you need before a verb to indicate an event will happen in the future?
   ....

5. Translate the following sentences:

   I am learning Mandarin.
   ....

   I am learning Chinese.
   ....

   I ate chicken today.
   ....

   [wǒ huì bāng nǐ]
   我会帮你。
   ....

List of Interrogative Pronouns

什么 [shén-me] = what

哪里 [ná-lǐ] = where

怎么(样) [zěn-me-(yàng)] = how

多少 [duō-shǎo] = how much

什么时候 [shén-me shí-hòu] = when

为什么 [wèi-shén-me] = why

谁 [shéi] = who

哪个 [nǎ-gè] = which (one)

Answer Key

Chapter 1

1. You are good. / You are well.
2. I am American. / I am from the U.S.
   You are Chinese? / You are from China?
   Rén
3. Wǒ shì xué
   Wǒ shì

Chapter 2

1. Wó/wǒ xiǎng yào (我想要)
2. Gè (个)
3. Xiǎng yào (想要)
4. I would like (some) milk tea.
   You would like (some) beef noodles?
5. Shén-me
6. Wó/wǒ xiǎng yào

Chapter 3

1. Zài (在)
2. Nǐ zài ná/nǎ-lǐ? (你在哪里？)
3. Yes
4. I am at the subway station.
   I am in front of the subway station.
   I am on the right side of the bus stop.
   I am on the east side of the bus stop.
5. Ní/nǐ xiǎng qù
   Wó/wǒ xiǎng qù

Part I Review

1. I am from Sichuan.
2. Wó/wǒ xiǎng yào yì-wán/wǎn hǎi-xiān miàn
3. Nǐ zài ná-lǐ

Chapter 4

1. Huì (会)
2. Liǎng (两)
3. Tā xiǎng yào liǎng-bēi kā-fēi (他想要两杯咖啡)
4. I worked here for two years.
   You worked at this place for five years?
5. 1 3 5 7 9
   2 4 6 8 10

Chapter 5

1. Dì (第)
2. Qù (去)
3. Bù (不)
4. Then
   Finally
5. Sān lù
   Dì tiě qī hào xiàn
   Nǐ yào zuò dì tiě èr hào xiàn

Chapter 6

1. Dōng-xi (东西)
2. De (的)
3. Yí-gòng duō-shǎo qián? (一共多少钱？)
4. I would like an admission ticket.
   Student ticket is ￥12.
   This is my student ID.
5. Liù kuài
   Shí-liù kuài
   Liù-shí-yī kuài

Part II Review

1. Niú ròu miàn duō shǎo qián? (牛肉面多少钱？)
2. Nǐ de niú ròu miàn duō shǎo qián? (你的牛肉面多少钱？)
3. Wǒ bú huì zhōng wén (我不会中文。)

Chapter 7

1. Xīng-qī (星期)
2. Subject-verb-object
3. Ní/nǐ xǐ-huān zuò shén-me? (你喜欢做什么？)
4. I like Chinese.
   I don't like to exercise.
   I don't like to go to work on weekends.
5. Xǐ huān
   Xǐ huān chī

Chapter 8

1. No
2. Tā shì shéi? (她是谁？)
   Ní/nǐ yǒu nán péng-yǒu ma? (你有男朋友吗？)
   Which one is your girlfriend?
   Who is your girlfriend?
3. Wó/wǒ yǒu
4. Wǒ méi-yǒu

Chapter 9

1. Year-month-day
2. No
3. When is your birthday?
   Wǒ de shēng-rì shì qī-yuè èr-shí-jiǔ hào (我的生日是7月29号。)
   Today is October 11th, 2018.
4. Jīn nián
   Zhè gè yuè

Part III Review

1. Nǐ zhōu mò xǐ huān kàn zhōng wén shū ma
2. I don't have a younger brother.
3. My younger sister's birthday is on April 29th.

Chapter 10

1. No
2. Le (了)
3. Zài (在)
4. Huì (会)
5. Wǒ zài xué pǔ-tōng-huà (我在学普通话。)
   Wǒ zài xué zhōng-wén (我在学中文。)
   Wǒ jīn-tiān chī le jī-ròu (我今天吃了鸡肉。)
   I will help you.

References

ISO (2015). ISO 7098 Information and Documentation – Romanization of Chinese.

Liu, Lening. "The current state of Chinese language." Teaching Chinese to Students of Other Languages. Beijing Language and Culture University. Jul. 2016. Lecture.

Sabine, Mark. Mandarin – Words of the World. Words of the World. The University of Nottingham. 25 Sept. 2013. Web. 16 Oct. 2018.

Tan, Amy. The Joy Luck Club. New York: Ballantine Books, 1989. Print.

"Ten Countries with The Largest Population in mid 2017 (in Millions)." Chart. Statista. Aug. 2018. Web.

Zhou, Youguang. Interview by CNTV. 语言学家: 周有光. China Central Television (CCTV). 24 Dec. 2014. Film.

Acknowledgements

Here are so many people whom I want to thank from my heart because this book would not have become a reality without your love and contribution.

To *Rose Fan Zhang*, for your beautiful voice recording set for this book, and for always answering my Mandarin questions for this book patiently and conscientiously.

To *June Pham*, for the simple and structured design of the book's layout to make reading this book fun and engaging.

To *Ruth Kevess-Cohen*, not only for editing my books, but also for your useful advice in order for me to provide as many resources as I can to the readers.

To *Kimberly Newell*, not only for copy-editing this book, but also for being a loyal reader and supportive friend.

To *Ben Ho*, for your humility as my first student, your steadfast encouragement, and your innovative support that helped InspirLang to develop continuously.

To the *Writing Center at Baruch College*, for the resources provided to me while editing my early drafts.

To *Jian Liu*, for your beautiful voice recording set for this book, and for your passion in Chinese teaching that is contagious.

To *my parents*, who will semantically understand the half of this book that is written in Chinese and be wise enough to guess the other half that is written in English: for your ultimate support and sacrifice in this country, so that I could become a better me.

To *Alison Cohen*, my lifelong teacher, friend, and inspiration, for your kindness and encouragement and for making me believe in myself and follow my heart to write this and every book that I have written.

To *all of my students*, for always reminding me that learning a new language as an adult is not easy, and for always teaching me how to become a better person.

About the Author

Jade Jia Ying Wu completed her Teaching Certificate Program in TESOL (Teaching English to Speakers of Other Languages) and TCSOL (Teaching Chinese to Speakers of Other Languages) from Teachers College, Columbia University and Beijing Language and Culture University in 2016. She has taught Chinese in classrooms of various sizes and to students of all ages, in both the U.S. and China.

Jade was born and raised in Guangdong, China, where Cantonese is one of the main dialects. She moved to Swartz Creek, Michigan at the age of 13 and spent most of her young adulthood living in New York City. Experiencing both Chinese and American cultures, she was often confused yet fascinated by the differences between them. In 2014, she created her website InspirLang to teach Cantonese, Mandarin, and Taishanese to non-native speakers, and developed her own Romanized system for Taishanese. She currently hosts three language podcasts: Learn Mandarin Daily, Learn Cantonese Daily, and Learn Taishanese Daily. She is also the author of *Learn to Speak Cantonese I: A Beginner's Guide to Mastering Conversational Cantonese*.

In her free time, Jade also enjoys learning other languages such as Spanish, Vietnamese and Korean. She resides in Brooklyn, New York.

Website: www.inspirlang.com
Youtube: www.youtube.com/c/inspirlang
Facebook: www.facebook.com/inspirlang
Twitter: www.twitter.com/inspirlang
RSS Feed: www.inspirlang.com/rssfeed

More from Jade

Learn to Speak Cantonese I
A beginner's guide to mastering conversational Cantonese
Jade Jia Ying Wu
ISBN 978-0-9996946-0-2

Imagine falling in love with someone, but not speaking the same language as their extended family. This is the case for Gabriel, the narrator of this textbook, who is an American boy learning Cantonese to impress his girlfriend's mom. In this Cantonese learning book, you will join Gabriel in his first meeting with Jenny's mother, who is from Hong Kong and can only speak Cantonese. From having dim sum to describing his favorite pastimes, Gabriel will teach you everything you need to know to master basic conversational Cantonese.

Free audio and flashcards downloadable from
www.inspirlang.com/resource

Learn to speak Cantonese I is available on Amazon for purchase!

Made in the USA
Coppell, TX
06 February 2020